LABYRINTH

An International Journal for Philosophy, Value Theory and Sociocultural Hermeneutics

Printed ISSN 2410-4817
Online ISSN 1561-8927

Vol. 17, No. 2, Winter 2015

HISTORY AND CHOICE:

JEAN-PAUL SARTRE 1905-2015

Axia Academic Publishers

Bibliographische Information der Deutschen Nationalbibliothek:
Die Deutsche Nationalbibliothek verzeichnet diese Publikation in der Deutschen
Nationalbibliographie, detaillierte bibliographische Daten sind im Internet unter
http://dnb.dnb.de aufrufbar.

Die wissenschaftliche und redaktionelle Arbeit wurde von der Kulturabteilung
der Stadt Wien – Wissenschafts- und Forschungsförderung unterstützt.

*Labyrinth: An International Journal for Philosophy, Value Theory and
Sociocultural Hermeneutics* is a serial publication of the Institut für Axiologische
Forschungen / Institute for Axiological Research, Vienna – www.iaf.ac.at
For more information please visit the Journal's homepage:
www.labyrinth.axiapublishers.com

LABYRINTH, Vol. 17, No. 2, Winter 2015

HISTORY AND CHOICE:
JEAN-PAUL SARTRE 1905-2015

CONTENTS

HISTORY AND CHOICE: JEAN-PAUL SARTRE 1905-2015

IN MEMORIAM

INTERVIEW

PETER CAWS (Washington)

On the Intelligibility of our Present History:
The Contemporary Relevance of the *Critique of Dialectical Reason* and some other Sartrian Texts

Abstract

Jean-Paul Sartre is the writer who gave the most trenchant formulation of existentialism and tried to do the same for a version of Marxism, and as a philosopher of history who got it wrong about history and then, in his last "philosophical manifesto" – volume III of the Idiot (English version volume V) – got it brilliantly right. But Sartre did not write the second volume of the Critique. Or, more exactly, he wrote it but he did not publish it. The Critique, as Sartre himself admitted, grew like a hernia on the body of the book on Flaubert, so that it had to be surgically removed and given a life of its own; but a sort of symbiosis persisted, and when it came to the continuation of the argument, Sartre seems to have sensed that volume II was a dead end, and that the route to the alternative would prove to lie after all in the Flaubert project itself. In order to understand Sartre's position, the author analyzes his conception of history, especially of the intelligibility of history by mean of the dialectical reason as a movement of totalization of practical seriality, and shows its actuality.

Keywords: Jean-Paul Sartre, Critique, Dialectics, Reason, History, Politics

Sartre's three major philosophical works deal respectively, to put things in their simplest terms, with being, with history, and with life – the last with a life lived by a particular being at a particular epoch of history. They all remain strikingly relevant to the beings that we are, living our lives in our own historical moment. It is a moment fraught with troubled uncertainty: where is our present history taking us? Guided by what leaders, towards what ends? I do not say towards what destiny, because that would introduce a historicist prejudice that I reject. And I use the term "leader" with a certain reserve, given Sartre's well-known attitude towards the very idea of a leader – yet there do exist individuals in positions of leadership, exerting the powers of those positions for ends of their own that may need also to be rejected, and resisted. What were Sartre's thoughts about history as such, and about the history he lived? What would he have said about the history we are living? What ought *we* to say about it?

In the course of this inquiry I will touch on other themes, especially on war and on terror. But I will begin anecdotally, and I ask for your indulgence in that regard. The anecdotes, personal as they are, will make a philosophical point, and that will lead me into the substance of what I want to say. Let me then tell you how, more than a quarter of a century ago, I did not meet Jean-Paul Sartre.

When in the middle 1970s I was writing my *Sartre* an old Paris acquaintance, Jean Pouillon, who was for many years Sartre's colleague at *Les temps modernes*, very kindly asked me if I would like to meet him. I would, of course – but when I thought about it the idea seemed somehow wrong. I knew Sartre through his work, and had made it my task to know the work thoroughly – the philosophical work, that is, not so much the novels and plays, though I obviously could not ignore them altogether. I knew him, therefore, in much the same way as I knew Descartes or Plato or Kant. Meeting great philosophers in the flesh can be disconcerting – they haven't the slightest idea who you are, and if in response to a benign inquiry you tell them you're writing about them the whole thing begins to seem banal (yet another academic: what's worse, one who teaches in America!). I was getting to know my Sartre, the writing one, pretty well, and knew what I wanted to say about him; I wondered if meeting the living one would somehow distort the philosophical image, or skew my rendering of it in the light of some casual remark that would take on disproportionate weight because of having come directly from the source. So I thanked Pouillon and said I thought I would wait until I had finished my book.

In due course the book was finished. I was spending a year in Paris and the Pouillons came to dinner; Jean Pouillon wanted to see it. On the cover of the books in the series for which I had written it – the Routledge "Arguments of the Philosophers" – the publishers had the idea of putting a sample of the handwriting of the philosopher in question; they had rung me up and asked if I could secure a sample of Sartre's handwriting, and I had found a dealer who had sold me a page or two, notes about the failure of the bourgeoisie to understand its rights and freedoms in any light other than as a license to oppress. Pouillon approved of the book – "but whose handwriting is this?" he asked. Certainly it was not Sartre's. He turned to Madame Pouillon, who happens to be a graphologist; definitely not Sartre's, she agreed. I had visions of public humiliation, of the recall of the entire edition for the re-design of the cover. Suddenly Madame Pouillon exclaimed – "It's Simone's!" And so it proved to be: my dealer was right about the provenance of the manuscript, wrong, in this case, about whose hand had written it. It seemed clear that Simone de Beauvoir had been helping Sartre, then becoming blind, in his inveterate habit of getting thoughts on to paper. (This detail may serve as a footnote to the story of the intellectual relations between Sartre and de Beauvoir – she wrote it, but was it only he who thought it?)

Now I was ready to meet Sartre. But I had waited too long. Do him a kindness, said Pouillon, don't ask to meet him now. "*Sartre n'est plus Sartre,*" Sartre is no longer Sartre – a wreck of his former self, he could hardly see and could not control some of his bodily functions, while eating, for example. It would be an embarrassment all around. Edward Said had reported to me just such a scene of painful awkwardness at a lunch he had attended, and it would obviously have been not merely pointless but also intrusive to on my part to insist. A few months later I was among the crowds that followed the coffin from the hospital to the cemetery – an enormous "series," in the language of the *Critique of Dialectical Reason*, turning for a few hours into a rather amorphous "group in fusion," seen as a collective agent certainly by impatient motorists who found themselves, with no idea of what was going on, immobilized by rivers of humanity. Given Sartre's known views on the authoritarian functions of the State it would have been inappropriate, according to his friends, to look for the help or approval of the police for this manifestation.

That, then, was the end of the Sartre I had not met. But it was not the end of *my* Sartre, who continued and continues to be just the author of the roughly ten thousand pages of philosophical writing he published during his lifetime. I had taken the risk in my book of claiming that it was now possible "to see Sartre's work as an essentially completed whole" (Caws 1979, 4), a claim that seemed to be vindicated when he died without producing any more of it. My Sartre was not the "*vieillard détourné,*" the old man led astray, whom many critics saw in the last Benny Lévy / Pierre Victor interviews, he was a living figure in the history of contemporary philosophy, whose place there was assured, I thought, if not for all time at least for any future in which philosophy as I knew it would survive.

Sartre's place in the history of philosophy – that I suppose is in part at least what we are here to commemorate. This language opens up a rich vein for reflection. To commemorate, to remember together: the place of memory between the event or the life and their respective histories is one of the topics I want to touch on in what follows. And another is the history of philosophy, contemporary or otherwise, in relation to yet other histories, personal or epochal, including notably our own, especially in the years since 2001 and those to come. Whose Sartre are we talking about? Without elaborating the underlying theory of the mode of being of cultural objects that justifies the assertion (something I'm happy to do on request) I will assert that everyone has his or her own Sartre, in the sense that no two of us have read just the same works, with the same patience or intensity, in the same order, even considering only those published before 1980, that we have different views about the inclusion of the posthumous works, and so on. Some know Sartre in French, others only or mainly through translations; some have focused principally on *Being and Nothingness*, some on the *Critique*, while others have actually worked all the way through *The Family Idiot*. (I cite titles in English, because this paper is written in English, but here I am talking equally about the French originals – and this is not a trivial point, since the major translations leave a lot to be desired, though I cannot speak for translations into languages other than English.)

Also, to come at last to my main topic, though by an indirect approach, everyone, in an analogous way, has his or her own history. History requires a subject, and a historian; the two are rarely the same, although in my view they start out that way. Each of us has his or her own personal history, more or less complete, more or less reliable (fabulation begins early); as I suggested just now, history is mediated by memory, but at some point we are no longer just remembering the facts about our own past actions and experiences, we have come to rely on the memories of others, but also on documents, on photographs, on possessions, on the enduring works of our hands or brains. And each of us is in one way or another a private historicist: our lives are on a trajectory from past to future, they involve an earlier and a later, recollection and anticipation. It is not that we recall our births or (if we follow Spinoza's advice) anticipate our deaths, indeed as I have remarked elsewhere lived human subjectivity is remarkable in that everything happens as if – from the point of view of the subject him- or herself – it *had* neither beginning nor end. (On reflection that proves to be the case for history in the larger sense too – or rather, history *need* have no beginning or end, it requires neither a myth of creation nor an eschatological myth, even though there are some histories – for example, that of the Roman Empire – which can be told from foundation to dissolution.) It is rather that we tend to order, or to try to order, our own lives as an unfolding story, in which events are dated, explainable and perhaps justifiable in terms of contingencies and purposes. All that history needs are two of the three categories that for Hume defined causality, namely contiguity and succession; into the fact that the third category, constant conjunction, cannot be expected of it can be packed the whole problematic of the philosophy of history.

The subject of my personal history is myself; the subject of the history of the Roman Empire is – the Roman Empire: whatever sort of object that is. The historian of my personal history, when I come to awareness of it *as* a history, is again, in the first instance, myself, though I may have helps in the early stages from doting parents and in later ones from official record-keepers and, if I rise to sufficient eminence, biographers. Who is the historian of the Roman Empire? To simplify the argument let us settle upon Gibbon. But Gibbon's history, as something living, can no longer count on him; what it requires is *us*, his readers; each of us, in reading Gibbon, becomes *pro tem* the historian of the Roman Empire or rather, not exactly *the* Roman Empire, but his or her Roman Empire. I mean no offense to professional historians when I condense these reflections into a maxim: *Only individuals have histories*. I remember that when I floated this idea with a colleague long ago she took me to mean that the only histories are the histories of individuals, rather as Emerson claims in his essay on History that "there is properly no history; only biography." But that was not at all what I meant. Individuals may start with their own histories, but they may also eventually "have" other histories – the history of the Roman Empire, the history of the Gulf War and its aftermath, the histories of science and technology, the history of philosophy – with Sartre in his place, whatever they may determine that to be.

I have told you who my Sartre is. He fits into my history of philosophy as the writer who gave the most trenchant formulation of existentialism and tried to do the same for a version of Marxism, and as a philosopher of history who got it wrong about history and then, in what I have called his last philosophical manifesto – volume III of the *Idiot*, or in the English version volume V – got it brilliantly right. No, this is not quite fair: he was on the way to getting it right in the first volume of the *Critique*; it was in the second volume that he went wrong. But my Sartre did not write the second volume of the *Critique*. Jean-Paul Sartre, the man I never met, wrote it, but he did not publish it. Granted, writing and not publishing is not the same as not writing – but still it is worth remembering a pointed remark in *Existentialism is a Humanism*: "Why say that Racine could have written another tragedy, when he didn't write it?" (Sartre 1947, 37-38). Suppose we were to adapt this to the *Critique*: "Why say that Sartre could have published another volume of the *Critique*, when he didn't publish it?"

Well, he couldn't publish it because it wasn't finished – so we'll publish it for him; that's what literary executors and devoted scholars do. But why wasn't it finished? I have touched on this problem elsewhere, in an article called "Posthumous Anachronisms in the Work of Sartre" (in Lee 1988: 363-374). The view I take there is that the published work forms a fairly consistent totality, culminating in the third volume of the *Idiot*, and that what remained unpublished was not so much repudiated as side-stepped. Sartre had a habit of referring to forthcoming publications – like the "*future work*" announced in the very last sentence of *Being and Nothingness* – which then failed to appear, not because he had abandoned the project but because it had found one or more alternative outlets, in that case *Saint Genet* and the essay on the Jewish Question. The *Critique*, as Sartre himself admitted, grew like a hernia on the body of the book on Flaubert, so that it had to be surgically removed and given a life of its own; but a sort of symbiosis persisted, and when it came to the continuation of the argument my Sartre seems to have sensed that volume II was a dead end, and that the route to the alternative would prove to lie after all in the Flaubert project itself.

(I may say parenthetically that my choice of a restricted Sartre implies no criticism of those who choose a more inclusive one, up to the "totalization" aimed at by Contat and Rybalka. It is a rich vineyard, with room for many workers.)

Unpacking all this requires some reflection on what, for Sartre, history consisted in. The subtitle chosen by its editors for the second volume of the *Critique* is *The Intelligibility of History*. Intelligibility is clearly a basic desideratum, but the subtitle requires explication with respect to both its terms: what (or whose) history is to be intelligible, what are the criteria for intelligibility? Some such desire seems to characterize the way many individuals think about their personal histories – they want their lives to be meaningful, to make sense in some larger scheme of things. I have called this "the delusion of meaning," suggesting that the quest for "the meaning of life" is doomed to failure, much as the quest for "the meaning of language" might be. The error is easier to see in the latter case: language as such doesn't have meaning, language makes meaning possible. The same is true of life: having life (the point seems almost too simple) is the condition for engaging in meaningful activities, our opportunity for the construction of meanings. The thing to aim for, I suggest, is not the meaning of life but a life of meaning – a life full of the meanings that reside in relations with others, in work, in art and literature and philosophy, in acquaintance with nature and the cultivation of skills and talents. *Living* such a life fully leaves us less liable to the futile search for overarching meanings, either of lives or of histories, that would derive their sense from elsewhere.

The need for a more global interpretation of one's own life, however, dies hard, and Sartre's own trajectory leads with it. He understands from the beginning – it is one of his trademarks, and the underlying theme of *Being and Nothingness* – the contingency of existence, but he wants to grapple with it, to dominate it. In a remarkable letter to Simone de Beauvoir he refers to the irrationalities into which the individual is thrown, and the natural tendency to *mask* them, which "means simply adopting an attitude of inauthenticity toward them." One of the irrationalities of his own life was the atmosphere of preparation for war.

> ... I realize I was in a state of total inauthenticity about that. I was masking it, and what I wasn't seeing was that our era (1918-1939) derives its meaning from nothing else (in its totality and its smallest details) but a being-for-the-war. So it seems to me for twenty years and at the very core of my nature I had, in spite of myself and unknowingly, an inauthentic being-for-the-war. What should have been done? To live and think this war on the horizon as a specific possibility of this era. Then I would have grasped my *historicity*, which was to be destined for this war (had it even been avoided in '39 and forever, it was no less the concrete meaning of the whole era). Of course, you shouldn't believe that this means I should have resigned myself to it or accepted it. But only considered it as my fate, understood that in *choosing* to be of this era, I was choosing myself for this war. You will answer: You didn't choose this era, you fell into it. No indeed [*Mais non* – that "indeed" mutes the challenge of this interjection]. I will explain that we chose it – and I don't mean that in the metaphysical sense of intelligible choice. But in the concrete sense (Sartre 1992, 315).

So he is looking for the meaning of the era, and also for his own historicity, his participation in that meaning by a concrete choice. There is something Nietzschean in his attitude, wishing to turn "thus it was" into "thus I willed it," after the manner of Zarathustra; also something Hegelian, freely choosing what will be shown to have been necessary. The Left Hegelian Marx is still for the most part in Sartre's future, though his message will clearly be welcome in due course. For the moment this embracing of the contingent as necessary is the key to the existentialist project: thrown forward, the for-itself rides its own facticity, and its good faith lies in its refusal to mask the stark givenness of its situation. And yet to introduce "being-for-war" as a category at the core of existence, to give histori-cal contingency such *ontological* weight, is surely to succumb to a youthful passion for intelligibility that mature reflection will curb. The point deserves a longer argument than there is time for here – it would turn on the relation between the subject and its project, and on what sense it makes to say that something ought to have been my project when it wasn't, but I must leave it for another occasion.

After the war, driven as much by a sharpened political awareness as by the inner de-velopment of his own thought, came Sartre's well-known turn towards Marxism. Happy neither with Moscow nor with Washington, he nevertheless aligned himself with socialism rather than capitalism, an obvious choice for someone with his experience and sympathies – and antipathies, for example towards the bourgeoisie. But with Marx came philosophical baggage that would encumber him for years. It has always seemed to me that Marx made a fortunate choice in following Feuerbach, an unfortunate one in following Hegel. "Dialecti-cal materialism" is an oxymoron, not as everyone knows directly attributable to Marx, but as a slogan to Plekhanov and as a theory (in the form of an impossible "dialectics of na-ture") to Engels. Historical materialism makes sense for limited episodes, involving cli-mate, scarcity, migration, technology and so on, and history, as understood by historians, can plausibly be given, often enough, a dialectical structure. But the attempt to invert He-gel's absolute and totalizing idealism, with its world-historical pretensions to intelligibility and completeness, and stand it on materialist feet, was as I see it doomed to failure from the beginning. The best model for the dialectic is Platonic, not Hegelian: beginning *in medias res,* and ending when the participants in the dialogue get tired and go home, it draws its philosophical power from its philosophical modesty. Applied to history, it can make sense of particular epochs and even particular contradictions and their particular *Aufhebungen*, but the attempt to embed these in any sort of total historical necessity represents a fatal overstepping of inherent limitations.

At the time of the *Critique* Sartre has not yet come to terms with these limitations; he is still under the spell of what might be called the "lure of totalization," and his project is to show how History (with a capital H) can be understood dialectically. Understanding is the work of reason, and dialectical reason, "the very movement of totalization," is the road to it for historical purposes. I have expressed elsewhere my reservations about this name –

it has sometimes seemed to me that Sartre chose it merely in order to have a title that would echo Kant's. I do not think it serves in any useful way to designate a special kind of reason ("pure reason" and "practical reason" in Kant represent different modalities, not different kinds), and it has led to pointless misunderstandings, notably in the controversy with Lévi-Strauss. So when I speak of the contemporary relevance of the *Critique of Dialectical Reason* I do not mean the relevance of the concept that gives the book its title, but the relevance of the arguments that the book contains.

The philosophical importance and the contemporary relevance of the *Critique* lie for me in the way in which Sartre works out the theory of the group. Like Marx, to whom he appeals in the prefatory *Problem of Method*, he wants to base his work on what is unequivocally given:

> We willingly grant that the group never has and never can have the type of metaphysical existence which people try to give to it. We repeat with Marxism: there are only men and real relations between men. From this point of view, the group is in one sense only a multiplicity of relations and of relations among those relations.

So the task of the book is to work out a theory that will explain how real individuals, each a free project, jointly produce an intelligible history. This involves a true dialectic, in that there is a progression from a neutral position, via practical seriality and the various stages of group formation, to a situation in which conflict emerges between individuals and institutions, between leaders and the rank-and-file, potentially between citizens and governments. It is a dialectic that has a cyclical form, repeating itself endlessly, not from some remote beginning to some remote end, but from a concrete situation to its equally concrete outcome. We are not condemned to this endless repetition – the very purpose of theory, after all, is to enable people to avoid predictable outcomes – but if we understand its likelihood we will be in a better position to develop strategies of avoidance.

The most significant lesson of this analysis seems to me to lie in Sartre's understanding of how revolutionary group practice emerges from a consciousness of seriality. It is a lesson we need to learn more urgently than ever, but one whose application is more difficult than ever. The secret of successful political repression (whether or not recognized under that name) is to ensure that the people constitute and continue to constitute a series – in relation to popular culture, to consumer markets, to communications, to the law, to governmental administration – that never rises to group awareness. The old way to break out of this bind, through the group-in-fusion and the sworn group, with its fraternity-terror, led all too quickly (in the history of Soviet politics, for example) to the emergence of an institutional elite and the consequent re-emergence of seriality. Sartre does not himself arrive at a new way, but he sets up the challenge for us. What he does offer is an exquisitely detailed set of observations of the process at work in particular social and political contexts.

It is a historical process, but its intelligibility shows through most convincingly in local rather than in global contexts: small totalizations rather than large ones. Even there history proves to be elusive. One of Sartre's vivid analyses traces the intelligible moves in the collective praxis of a game of football, and a great moment of comic (but at the same time profound) insight comes in a wry footnote to this account: "In fact, in a football match, everything is complicated by the presence of the opposite team" (Sartre 1976, 473). (The enveloping structure of organized competition is further worked out early in the second volume with his account of the world of boxing.) The dream of final totalization is thwarted by such considerations – the dialectic unfolds smoothly only as long as it is a collaborative process, but (as Engels realized long ago) there are too many conflicting projects and desires to permit any sort of rational outcome on the largest scale.

That is why the project of the second volume, the intelligibility of history in some all-encompassing sense, has to be abandoned. While the first volume ends with what seems to me a desperate gesture towards what Sartre calls "totalization without a totalizer," the second aims at the much more ambitious concept of a "totalization of envelopment," in the light of which the whole course of human events might fall into place. The problem with such a grandiose history, of the world, of mankind, is that it lacks a specifiable subject. The candidate for the status of such a subject, in the Marxist historicism of the Critique (and in the name of the French Communist daily), is "Humanity," but as Sartre eventually comes to see

> ... humanity *is not* and does not respond diachronically to any concept; what does exist is an infinite series whose law is recurrence, defined precisely in these terms: man is the son of man. For this reason history is perpetually finite, composed of broken sequences, each of which is the *deviated* (not mechanically but dialectically) continuation of the one before as well as the surpassing of that preceding sequence toward ends that are the *same* and *other* ... (Sartre 1994, 403-404)

According to this view histories (in the plural) would be relatively local; they would have the sense we give them, we would not be inclined to think that they had to be part of some cosmic venture, some destiny of mankind, some working-out of Providential purposes. Such a view has immediate and useful implications for our understanding of current events.

Combining the theory of groups with this somewhat chastened theory of history we can read the present world situation as one of massive seriality, maintained by the technology of dissemination, in which institutional hierarchies, mainly fundamentalist in tendency, manipulate their respective (serialized) publics in order to implement their own conflicting visions of world history, driven by ambitions of economic and ideological domination. These visions are delusional, and criminally dangerous. A general realization, on the part of a sufficient number of individual subjects, of their condition of exploited seriality, and at the same time of the emptiness of the world-historical schemas that drive the conflicts into which they are repeatedly drawn, would undercut this situation. The powers that profit from it cannot allow this to happen. It is to Sartre's credit that he was willing to be convinced, in the end, of the emptiness of the Marxist schema in which he had invested such energy and such hope. But where did that leave him in relation to the history of his own epoch?

World War II was not Sartre's only war. The two others in which his interest and influence were engaged were the Algerian war of 1954-1962 and the Vietnam war of 1964-1975. In effect there is also a third: the (potential) World War III that seemed to loom so imminently in the late 1940s. In speaking of them he no longer invokes being-for war but goes more deeply into the social, psychological, and political causes and by-products of conflict. What he finds, and what he says, tally so closely with some of the issues involved in our contemporary wars – the phony one and the real one – that I shall take the liberty of dealing with them all as variants on a common theme. By the phony war I mean of course the so-called "war on terror" (2001 to date), and by the real one the shamefully one-sided Iraq war (2003 to date). All these wars were embedded in histories: the history of colonialism, the history of anticommunism, the history of nuclear armaments, the history of radical Islam, the history of the technology of petroleum. To understand this embedding a few more remarks on history – not directly influenced by Sartre – are in order.

I sometimes find it useful to talk about two kinds of history, which I will call history 1 and history 2. History 1 isn't really history at all, although it is what a lot of people seem to mean when they use the term – it is whatever "really happens," as it happens, as if this were something frozen and could be recaptured. History 2 is what we say about what happened, how we connect it to other things that happened, how we categorize it, how we explain it. History 1 is over as soon as it has happened; history 2 can begin only when memory has done its preliminary work of recognition and comparison. History 1 is given, if you can catch it; history 2 is chosen, not as to its basis in events but as to its structure in their mutual relations. Consider what is generally taken to have been the defining event of our recent history, the attack on the World Trade towers on September 11, 2001. As history 1 it was indeed captured, in multiple and endlessly recirculated images, images which live in the memory of millions of people who, thanks to the media, witnessed it at a distance. But what sort of event was it? An outright act of war? A criminal act? A brilliant guerrilla stroke carried into enemy territory? And to what history 2 does it belong? To the history of fundamentalist alienation, to the history of American imperialism, or to some other history, of aviation or of urbanization for example?

In fact the event clearly belongs to all those histories, and more. But what happened was that it was instantly inscribed, by the President of the United States, in a fantastic history of pure but embattled democracy as an object of primitive resentment and hatred. He chose to construe it as an act of war that instantly and unilaterally put the government of the United States on a war footing, even though according to its Constitution the country cannot be placed in such a position except by a declaration, after due deliberation, on the part of Congress. No serious opportunity was afforded for such deliberation, and no such declaration was ever made. The war was to be a "war on terror," and under that name it has cost so far something on the order of a hundred thousand unnecessary deaths and two hundred billion unnecessary dollars. The choice of this particular history, backed by another and even more fateful choice – that of one of the oldest of mythical historicisms, apocalyptic Christianity – may prove to have been the defining tragedy of our time.

Terror is an exaggerated form of fear, and the war on terror has played on the fears of the American people, unaccustomed as they are to threats at home. Terrorism depends for its success on inspiring fear, and those who encourage fear, who use it to whip up wrath against enemies, real or imagined, are really doing the terrorists' work. Sartre calls them "*imbéciles*," and that seems singularly appropriate: Latin *imbecillus* meant originally physical weakness, possibly even (conjecturally) unreadiness for war, but it came to mean "lacking intellectual or moral strength." Sartre knew something about terror, and about fear – what would he have said about these developments? Extreme fear has its place, for him, in the emergence of some (though surely not all) groups, when their survival is at risk and members in effect put their lives in one another's hands; this is the "fraternity-terror" of the *Critique*, which comes into play when I swear that, if I fail my brothers, they may kill me. In the present context, though, the *Critique* is not perhaps the most relevant text (even though it does contain an analysis of the concept of Terror, especially in relation to the French revolution, in which however Sartre points out that the concept corresponds to no single essence (Sartre 1976, 597n)).

His thoughts about fear surface most prominently in his reflections about the dangers of World War III, those about terror (in its contemporary political sense) in his reflections on the Algerian war, notably in the preface to Fanon's *The Wretched of the Earth*. In both cases succumbing to the threat is both a consequence and a cause of dehumanization. "This war will be the war of fear," he writes in 1946:

> ... if we keep on waiting for it all this time, if we have to souse ourselves in fear for fifty years, if we convince ourselves that we must wait until the coming war is over before we can start living, then we will have made the Bomb three-quarters useless: there will not be any men left to kill; that will have been done already (Contat and Rybalka 1974/1, 157).

The sinister thing about this fear is the policies it will provoke in governments that fall prey to it, the carnage that will follow if they use their technological power to conduct war at a distance:

> Then the abstract massacre will start. ... Technicians off in Washington and Texas will
> set up a slaughterhouse in Baku or in Leningrad and never even see it. Never even imag-
> ine it. No heroes; no martyrs: just a cataclysm coming down on panic-stricken animals
> (*ibid.*).

Change Baku and Leningrad to Baghdad and Fallujah, change technicians to politicians – but we don't even have to change Washington or Texas. Granted that our present war
is not the nuclear war about which Sartre was writing; granted that there is still some combat
on the ground – but the shock and awe of overwhelming firepower are as morally repugnant
now as the idea of the bomb was then.

In this and other texts of the post-World War II period one cannot help being struck by
the way in which the fear that pervaded society then because of the Communist threat antici-
pates the fear that pervades our own society now (I speak principally for the United States)
because of the terrorist threat. Fear of the Soviet Union fueled American anti-communism in
the fifties, fear of Al Qaeda fuels American anti-terrorism in the present decades. The current
version is the more pathetically disproportionate to the threat, empowering as it does a small
group of essentially stateless outlaws who happen to have pulled off one dramatic, brilliant,
large scale, and thanks to the media very public coup against the image of the corporate West,
and who have been allowed thereby to determine the economic future of the world's thereto-
fore richest and most powerful state. That this was, abstractly regarded, an evil act hardly
needs arguing, but then evil acts abound, and Sartre would certainly want to remind us of this:
their evil does not excuse our evil, we cannot expect to go unscathed.

In the context of the Algerian war it is not that Sartre condones terror – he simply
points out that those who rule by terror can expect to be repaid in terror. His description of the
colonial oppressor is merciless:

> ... this imperious being, crazed by his absolute power and by the fear of losing it, no
> longer remembers clearly that he was once a man; he takes himself for a horsewhip or a
> gun; he has come to believe that the domestication of the "inferior races" will come
> about by the conditioning of their reflexes. But in this he leaves out of account the hu-
> man memory and the ineffaceable marks left upon it; and then, above all, there is some-
> thing which perhaps he has never known: we only become what we are by the radical
> and deep-seated refusal of that which others have made of us. .... [T]hese constantly re-
> newed aggressions, far from bringing them to submission, thrust them into an unbeara-
> ble contradiction which the European will pay for sooner or later (Fanon 1968,16).

Once again, under a fairly obvious application of the rule of *mutatis mutandis*, the
relevance of this passage to our present history is clear enough. The futility of a policy of

"constantly renewed aggressions" on the part of leaders who put their confidence in military, rather than in intellectual or moral, strength, ought by now to be apparent.

Would Sartre be able to do anything more about this now than he was able to do at the time of Vietnam, for example? If the leaders were unreachable then, they seem even more so now. We can at least be sure that if Sartre were alive today he would be ready to convoke an "Iraq tribunal" along the lines of the Russell Vietnam tribunal. (But who corresponds to Russell today? And who to Sartre?) I will cite in conclusion what he said at the opening session of the Russell tribunal:

> In truth, we would wish, with press collaboration, to maintain constant contact between ourselves and the masses all over the world who are painfully watching the tragedy in Vietnam. We hope that they will be learning while we learn, that they will watch and understand, and come to their own conclusions. .... It is for the peoples of the world and, in particular, the American people that we are working (Sartre 1968).

"The American people": as an adopted American I once again ask for your indulgence, this time for bringing the burden of an American conscience to this celebration. But Sartre would have understood. In fact he often expressed such solidarity with the American people. In a text from 1948 on the looming struggle between the USA and the USSR ("We Must Have Peace to Remake the World') he says:

> We could not possibly conceive of ourselves fighting a democratic people who have often shown an admirable sense of freedom. It is true that this sense is being lost, but it is being lost to the extent that the United States is afraid a war will start and is getting ready for it (Contat and Rybalka 1974/2, 194).

Two more strikingly prescient texts, reading "Iraq" for "Vietnam" in the first and modifying the second to indicate that the United States is afraid a war has already started.

As I said above, the conclusion that we are at war depends on our choice of a history, and Sartre would undoubtedly join me in repudiating the choice that some of our leaders have made for us. He would have us choose a history based on freedom rather than on fear – freedom not simply from the threat of others, and not simply for unrestrained consumption and selfish satisfaction, but for the openness of the future to human projects, individual or collective, in mutual respect and for mutual welfare. To work towards such a history would be the most fitting tribute to his memory.

Prof. Dr. Peter Caws, George Washington University, pcaws@gwu.edu

References

Caws, Peter. *Sartre*. London: Routledge and Kegan Paul, 1979.

Contat, Michel and Rybalka, Michel. *The Writings of Jean-Paul Sartre*, vol. 1. Evanston: Northwestern University Press, 1974.

Contat, Michel and Rybalka, Michel. *The Writings of Jean-Paul Sartre*, vol. 2. Evanston: Northwestern University Press, 1974.

Fanon, Frantz. *The Wretched of the World*. Translated from the French by Richard Philcox with commentary by Jean-Paul Sartre and Homi K. Bhabha, 1968.

Lee, Sander H. (ed.), *Inquiries into Values*. Lewiston: Edwin Mellen Press, 1988.

Sartre, Jean-Paul. *Existentialism*. Translated by Bernard Frechtman. New York: Philosophical Library, 1947.

Sartre, Jean-Paul, "Inaugural Statement," in Against the Crime of Silence: Proceedings of the Russell International War Crimes Tribunal. New York: O'hare Books, 1968 (retrieved also online, 20 dec. 2015: http://raetowest.org/vietnam-war-crimes/russell-vietnam-war-crimes-tribunal-1967.html).

Sartre, Jean-Paul. *Critique of Dialectical Reason*. Translated by Alan Sheridan-Smith. London: New Left Books, 1976.

Sartre, Jean-Paul. *Witness to my Life: The Letters of Jean-Paul Sartre to Simone de Beauvoir, 1926-1939*. Edited by Simone de Beauvoir, translated by Lee Fahnestock and Norman MacAfee. New York: Scribner's, 1992.

Sartre, Jean-Paul. *The Family Idiot: Gustave Flaubert 1821-1857*. Vol. 5. Chicago: University of Chicago Press, 1994.

ERIK M. VOGT (Hartford/Vienna)

Some Notes (with Badiou and Žižek) on Event/Truth/Subject/Militant Community in Jean-Paul Sartre's Political Thought

Abstract

The main object of this paper is to examine the new philosophical frame proposed by Alain Badiou and Slavoj Žižek and to show that it implies some traces of Sartre's philosophical and political heritage. According the project of Alain Badiou and Slavoj Žižek one should no longer accept today's constellation of freedom, particularistic truth and democracy, but to (re)inscribe the issues of freedom and universal truth into a political project that attempts to re-activate a thinking of revolution. Their thinking consists in the wager that it is still possible to provide a philosophical frame for this leftist emancipatory position that claims the dimension of the universal against the vicious circle of capitalist globalization-cum-particularization and, by following Marx's claim that there are formal affinities between the ambitions of emancipatory politics and the working mode of capitalism, takes up the struggle of universalism against globalization (capital). It is only through this struggle for the universal that the intertwined processes of a constant expansion of the automatism of capital and "a process of fragmentation into closed identities," accompanied by "the culturalist and relativist ideology" (Badiou) can be suspended. It is precisely this constellation of revolutionary act, universal truth, subject, and militant community, that reveal some similarities with Sartre's concepts of the subject, the revolutionary action, the militant community a.o.

Keywords: Jean-Paul Sartre, Alain Badiou, Slavoj Žižek, political philosophy, subject, revolutionary action, militant community

In his "L'aveu du philosophe," Alain Badiou remarks upon the "moral mania" of modern biographies:

> I know of only three goals that they pursue (...)

The political goal: it has to be proven that the portrayed unfortunate man got involved with the totalitarian, that he was a bad democrat. This is, by the way, the reason why he got big, although one is supposed to remain little.

The financial goal: it has to be proven that he had a suspicious relationship towards money: Either he loved it too much, which is bad, or he loved it too little, which is even worse. Thus he has created fictions not for sale either through the sublimation of his greed or through the mirroring of his miserliness.

The supreme goal: the sexual goal the whole world is waiting for. It has to be demonstrated that he had disgusting manners. The relationship to his sexual victims – men, women, or even rabbits – was not rectified through politics. Or there is nothing to report, which is worse: he had no freedom, he was in a fix, and that is why he pursued abstraction."

Badiou then gives the following advice:

(…) attempt to escape biography while still alive, and throw as many sticks as possible between the wheels for the time after your death. Before your have become senile, burn the photographs of naked women in garters, the bank statements and your stock of pamphlets and manifestoes. (Badiou 2003a, 121 – 123; my translation)

As we know, Sartre did not heed this advice; he could not or did not want to heed it. For this reason it is not surprising that one finds in one of the most recent biography on him – Bernard-Henri Lévy's *Sartre. The Philosopher of the Twentieth Century* – sections with titles such as "Sartre and women" or "Sartre and money." However, what carries more weight is the fact that this biography describes Sartre's political actions at best as violations of human rights – of human rights for whose articulation, preservation, and dissemination this "New Philosopher" credits himself -, and at worst as totalitarian crime. Under recurring denunciations of Sartre's political actions and thought as "obsession," "pure madness" (Bernard-Henri Lévy 2003, 342), "self-hatred" (ibid.), "Stalinism," (ibid., 330) and "totalitarianism" – after all, "Marxism, for us, the cause is an open and shut case. For us, the children of the century now ended, the witnesses or clerks of its bloody balance-sheet, for us who now have at their disposal all the pieces of that macabre account, the time of illusion is, fortunately, over. Stalin was already in Lenin. Lenin was already in Marx" (ibid., 360) – the political legacy of Sartre is rendered illegible between an allegedly non-political Sartrean literature and literary theory, and a fashionable ethicization of Sartre – "Sartre with Levinas" – by means of a "Thermidorean" process, that is, a disarticulation separating Sartrean political activism from "every principle and every situation," while pretending "that this activism was ever only connected with the Chinese or Soviet States." "Once severed from its real content, 'leftist' activism (…) is filed alongside subjective pathology and fascination with totalitarian statism, a classification that does render it absolutely unintelligible." (Badiou 2005, 135-136) In short, this denial of political thought, its abdication under the sign of liberal democracy, of human rights and a humanitarian individualist morality, intends to dump the political sequences that Sartre had attempted to elaborate (French Revolution, Commune, Bolshevist Revolution) into some permanent unthinkable.

One would have to remark at length on this alleged "end of illusion"; what hides behind it is "the end of political utopias"; for today, one lives in the post-utopian time of pragmatic administration, of human rights with its apriori identified evil, and of liberal democracy, since one (particularly the "New Philosophers") has learned the hard lesson as to how noble utopias end up in totalitarian terror. What Lévy conveniently fails to mention is that his affirmation of post-politics is articulated precisely on the basis of the last great utopia: the utopia of capitalist liberal democracy as "end of history." However, in the face of current political conflicts one could ask whether the claim, that we live after the end of all utopias at the end of history, does not itself present the ultimate utopia. (Žižek 2004, 122-124)

What is more, the postmodern sophists have told us for some time now that the "grand narratives" have come to an end and that one finally finds oneself in the space of post-ideology. For can one not hold universal truth-claims articulated and actualized in the field of politics accountable for all catastrophes of recent history? Do they not explain sufficiently (and bury) the sequence revolution-totalitarianism? Today, truth as well as ideology critique must no longer figure in the horizon of politics and political theory. And philosophy must no longer think politics; rather, it has to defend the allegedly undamaged figure of liberal democracy. In other words, philosophy today is supposed to restrict itself to appeals to and apologies of liberal democracy. But precisely these appeals and apologies announcing the "good news" of the end of all ideology and ideology critique are nothing but ideology *par excellence*: they conceal their philosophical-political moment *as* ideologies precisely in their defense of liberal democracy.

This ubiquitous, shameless celebration of liberal democracy reveals, moreover, a fundamental alliance with a culture of complaint, with discourses of victimization, and a critique of "ethical violence" marking a variety of contemporary philosophies. They all seem to agree that the "fundamental evil" of traditional, metaphysical thought consists in its reduction of otherness to sameness. Consequently, philosophical thought today has to engage in exercises of humility so as to open up a space for evocations of some radical ethical Other.

Consequently, "true evil" has been displaced from capitalist exploitation to "ethnic fundamentalism" (the obscene underside of an ethics of difference), to "totalitarian violence" (the obscene underside of the doctrine of human rights and of humanitarianism), or, generally, to each collective political project that does not simply toe the line with liberal democracy. The enthusiastic denunciation of these "versions of criminal or barbarian evil," its alleged protection of liberal rights under the aegis of a claim regarding the fundamental "vulnerability" of the human being, obscures the fact that this denunciation functions as a prohibition to – at least think - true emancipation.

These ideologies form the pillars for the hegemonic liberal democratic system that provides comfort to postmodern "leftist" politicians (and political theorists) and the apostles of cultural studies. If one even still finds gestures of anti-capitalism, they are always already rendered harmless by the omnipresent horizon of liberal parliamentary democracy. That is, their challenge to a logic of exclusion or excommunication in the realm of politics for the sake of an agonistic plenitude of "others" is owed to a foreclosure of some antagonism that becomes visible, only if one identifies and renders problematic liberal parliamentary democracy as the political form of capitalism (as well as of its mirror-image: anticapitalism of pure politics). This means, however, that one should no longer accept today's constellation of freedom, particularistic truth and democracy, but that one has to (re)inscribe the issues of freedom and universal truth into a political project that attempts to re-activate a thinking of revolution. This is the project of Alain Badiou and Slavoj Žižek. Their thinking consists in the wager that it is still possible to provide a philosophical frame for this leftist emancipatory position that claims the dimension of the universal against the vicious circle of capitalist globalization-cum-particularization and, by following Marx's claim that there are formal affinities between the ambitions of emancipatory politics and the working mode of capitalism, takes up the struggle of universalism against globalization (capital). It is only through this struggle for the universal that the intertwined processes of a constant expansion of the automatism of capital and "a process of fragmentation into closed identities," accompanied by "the culturalist and relativist ideology" (Badiou 2003, 10) can be suspended.

Now, what is this new philosophical frame? To simplify matters: it consists of a constellation of revolutionary event or act, universal truth, subject, and militant community. And precisely in this constellation one can find – this is the wager of my essay – traces of Sartre's philosophical and political heritage.

In a first step, let us employ Žižek's schematizing of six different forms of political organization – a schematizing that constitutes an expansion of Jacques Rançiere's distinction between three figures of political philosophy: arche-politics, para-politics, and meta-politics (Rançiere 1998) – in order to mark negatively certain affinities between Sartre's political thought and that of Žižek and Badiou. Briefly put, the proper antagonistic logic of the political is denied in the first five figures of political philosophy – they are incompatible with Žižek's, Badiou's, and Sartre's revolutionary politics -, whereas only the sixth one will acknowledge it. While arche-politics operates with a communitarian approach whose basis is the model of closed, organic communities that want to find their voice and claim their particular identity (think of Sartre's critique of hyper-organism that imputes the ontological status of totality or of a collective subject to a group or community), para-politics reformulates political antagonism in terms of a de-politicized compliance with rules, an agonistic litigious process (recall that in *Critique of Dialectical Reason* Sartre makes clear that neither liberalism nor communitarian thought can think the radical political decision; and he is opposed as well to procedural or consensual conceptions of justice and morality since they presuppose what is untenable for Sartre: "(…) that different individuals or groups, with different horizons, and with characters and habits of totally different kinds, realise a contractual agreement in reciprocity *on a minimum basis*." (Sartre 2004, 531)[1] A political theory whose central term is "consensus" has to amount to a denial of the real antagonism because it has already anticipated this denial in a theoretical manner by positing, in form of a repetition, as its premise the metaphor of society as mere agonism. And precisely here one finds the very fissures revealing each transformation of antagonism into agonism as mere myth). Ultra-politics – one could think of Carl Schmitt's *The Concept of the Political* – presents a false radicalization of the political conflict since it reduces it to a warfare between a homogeneous national community and its "external" enemy: it displaces antagonism into the outside (see Sartre's trenchant critique – in *The Childhood of a Leader* and in *Anti-Semite and Jew* – of the visions of an organicist, closed, homogeneous (and, for this very reason, anti-Semitic) French society). Socialist meta-politics, on the other hand, reduces political antagonism to an economism, renders the political as mere semblance (think of Sartre's near ubiquitous critique of economic determinism). However, one has to point out with Žižek that the Marxist term "political economy" is more ambiguous since it "also opens up the space for the opposite gesture of introducing politics into the very heart of the economy, that is it denounces the very 'apolitical' character of the economic processes as the supreme ideological illusion" (Žižek 2001, 241) – a position that is close to Sartre's insistence that the political and the economic are intertwined and that one has to politicize the economic because neither the political nor the economic are completely autonomous.[2]

---

[1] See also my book *Sartres Wider-holung* (Vogt 1995, 210-212).
[2] This "symbolic" relation between the political and the economic (and the psychical) has interesting implications for the way in which Sartre's logic conceives the relation between particular and universal. Fredric Jameson remarks: "Implied in this is a whole new logic as well, in which the static model of the relationship of universal and particular would be replaced by one in which each particularity

Finally, post-politics operates with a liberal democratic model of negotiation and integration of the different strategic interests; it denies on the one hand that liberal democratic processes of decision are the form of the imperatives of capitalism, that is, that participation in the post-political process amounts ultimately to Sartre's "idiot's traps" (elections) in "capital parliamentarism" (Badiou) that Žižek illustrates again and again via the example of a button in an elevator that, if one presses it to close the door, has, however, no real effect; in post-politics, on the other hand, "the conflict of global ideological visions embodied in different parties which compete for power is replaced by the collaboration of enlightened technocrats (economists, public opinion specialists …) and liberal multiculturalists." (Žižek 2000, 198) Public opinion, expert knowledge etc. are, however, incompatible with the notion of truth in Badiou and in the later Sartre because they represent forms of epistemic alterity. I have attempted to show elsewhere how Sartre's analysis of racism and multiculturalism can be linked to Žižek's (and Badiou's) claim that the liberal democratic, multicultural gaze whose humanitarian figure and extensive "good nature" wants to bestow charity, goodness, and humanity on all forms of ethnic identity – think, for instance, of the figure of the "democrat" in Sartre's *Anti-Semite and Jew* ("No doubt, he proclaims that all men have equal rights; no doubt he has founded the League for the Rights of Men," but for this very reason, one can detect in the "most liberal democrat a tinge of anti-Semitism") – represents a disavowed form of reflexive racism. (Sartre 1948, 55 and 57)[3] For the plea for multicul-

---

symbolized realizes in itself and in its own mode the totality of the universal in question." (See Jameson 1971, 225).

[3] See my book *Sartres Wieder-holung* (Vogt 1995, 210-212). For a comparison of Sartre's and Žižek's analyses of racism and multiculturalism see my *Zugänge zur politischen Ästhetik* (Vogt 2003, 101-124). Incidentally, this allows also for a different reading of Sartre's "notorious" preface to Frantz Fanon's *The Wretched of the Earth*. This preface is not addressed to Africans, but rather exclusively to Europeans; Sartre does not attempt, on the basis of a "transcendental Europe," to prescribe or suggest to Africans what they would have to do regarding their liberation: Sartre's position is that of a listener, of a listener whose listening far exceeds the typical (multiculturalist) narcissism that listens to others only in so far as they contribute to the European ego-ideal. Moreover, Sartre does not impose liberal democratic principles on the African discourse of liberation and decolonization: he does not make any distinctions between democratic and "non-demoratic," "fundamentalist" options. I follow here closely Bruce Baugh's "Sartre, Derrida, and Commitment: The Case of Algeria," (Baugh 2003, 40, 16). Similarly, Badiou writes in *Ethics*: "Our suspicions are first aroused when we see that the self-declared apostles of ethics and of the ,right to difference' are clearly *horrified by any vigorously sustained difference*. For them, African customs are barbaric, Muslims are dreadful, the Chinese are totalitarian, and so on. As a matter of fact, this celebrated ,other' is acceptable only if he is a *good* other – which is to say what, exactly, if not *the same as us*? Respect for differences, of course! But on condition that the different be parliamentary-democratic, pro free-market economics, in favour of freedom of opinion, feminism, the environment… That is to say: I respect differences, but only, of course, in so far as that which differs also respects, just as I do, the said differences. Just as there can be, no freedom for

tural respect of differences conceals an identitarian logic of exclusion. As long as the other acts in accordance with our own values, we respect her; as long as we can identify ourselves with our differences and love to respect, the other is a "good" other; as soon as the cultural customs of the other are in conflict with our democratic pluralist values, she becomes an "evil" other.

Democratic multiculturalist pluralism can tolerate only itself; its moral consensus is an apriori fact, it relies upon a disavowed political decision; for even if post-politics acts like the management of a rational consensus respecting differences, it is and remains a political decision, in so far as its difference between "rational" and irrational" doctrines constitutes a political decision.

However, what is the sixth form of political organization, or proper politics? It is located in the very moment when revolution is "in the air" and everything is about to change. It is only in that very moment that truth can appear: the truth of fighting for a new society that emerges from those singular elements subverting the existing order. Those singular elements cannot be regarded as belonging to a particular set, and it is for this very reason that they are universally equal. Each of these elements renders universal equality and, at the same time, all particular identities indifferent. This truth of universal equality affirmed by those singular elements lacks representation: it constitutes an empty set; and precisely this empty set can subvert the established order and render contingency as the very site at which a new truth can emerge – and "revolution" designates the actualization of the empty, abstract universal set.[4]

Event

The revolutionary experience of the event implies the discovery of a truth: the truth of a situation, of a truth that is not *of* this situation. This truth, which is one and which has to count for all, is not a factual truth, but rather one that requires the transformation of what has counted so far as "facts." It is a truth for which one has to struggle, a truth that appears only in the context of an unconditional commitment, of a decision for it. This truth can never be glimpsed from the perspective of a neutral, historicist gaze.

---

the enemies of freedom', so there can be no respect for those whose difference consists precisely in not respecting differences. To prove the point, just consider the obsessive resentment expressed by the partisans of ethics regarding anything that resembles an Islamic ,fundamentalist'." (Badiou 2001, 24).
[4] I draw here heavily on Marc de Kesel's excellent summary of Badiou's "mathematical" rendition of the French Revolution (see de Kesel, 2004, 167 – 197).

In other words, the event has no objective content verifiable through "facts"; it cannot be calculated or predicted because it decides on all measures. There is no already established frame for the event; on the contrary, all already established frames are suspended by the event. Although it results from a situation, from a configuration of being, it can never be deduced from it. A radical caesura, it resembles (in certain but not all respects) Žižek's *act*, in so far as the act is also conceived as the suspension of an existing order, that is, as something without any support in that order. When seen from the standpoint of the status quo, it appears as surplus, as excess, as something impossible within the framework of the existing symbolic order. (Žižek 2000, 236)

The same applies to Sartre's (political-historical) revolutionary event, in so far as it is equally conceived as disorder, as rupture, explosion, and flash of lightning. Both in Badiou and Sartre one finds the claim regarding the fundamental link between event and contingency: "the event always is presented as having an underlying contingency because it includes chance." (Sartre 2005, 35) Moreover, it is interesting that the event receives one of its central figurations from literature. As Jameson points out, this notion of the revolutionary event is comprehended best in terms of literary categories. (Jameson 1971, 58) In order to illustrate this claim, let us briefly condense some of those traits of the literary work of art as event that Sartre develops in *What Is Literature?*

The literary work of art constitutes "a new event" that cannot be reduced to something given prior to it. (Sartre 1988, 54) It also cannot be explained by or reduced to the intentionalities or projects of its subjects (author, reader); rather, the literary work of art is a self-abandonment and self-sacrifice of both author and reader generating a metamorphosis: a self-sacrifice via "commitment, oath, (…), fidelity (…), constantly renewed choice." (Sartre 1988, 60)

The event of literature thus receives its status through a kind of self-abandonment that requires a certain violent work on one's self; it constitutes a challenge to projects, to utility, instrumentality; it is a performative speech-act, that is, an appeal to freedom: "it is a break, a refusal (…) of narcissism (…), an affirmation of negativity (…). Therefore, it is, if it springs up within the universe of desire, deliverance from the universe of desire. It is (…) an affirmation of interhuman relations." (Sartre 1992, 369) This "affirmation of interhuman relations," this mutual recognition of freedoms (of author and audience) introduces an excessive economy without limit, except that of freedom. What becomes manifest in the literary event is an experience of freedom; it marks a space of free invention.

With regard to the acts of writing and reading, the event of literature seems then to imply a kind of symbolic death of the subjects (author/reader) that produces an excess in which, so to speak, more is given than can be given. The event of literature opens up a community, a common discourse, emerging in the midst of the self-destruction of symbolic identities. What is given in this excessive event? A new communal relationship of exposed subjects.

Thus the structure of the literary event carries, perhaps, within itself the model for a new political community: Sartre writes: "(…) literature will be a synthesis of negativity, as a power of uprooting from the given, … it will be the festival, the flaming mirror which burns everything reflected in it, and generosity, that is, a free invention, a gift. (…) In short, literature is, in essence, the subjectivity of a society in permanent revolution. In such a society it would go beyond the antinomy of word and action." (Sartre 1988, 139) Consequently, one could claim that Sartre's artistic practice has its own revolutionary politics, and it is now the task of revolutionary politics to appropriate for its own use the very modes of presentation that have been produced through this artistic practice.

Sartre's identification of literary and political event, the identity of word and action – do these not call to mind another confluence of the essence of literature with the properly revolutionary moment, namely Maurice Blanchot's account of the literary act and of revolutionary action in his "Literature and the Right to Death"? Consider the following passage from this text which maintains about revolutionary moments that they are

> in fact, fabulous moments: in them, fable speaks; in them, speech of fable becomes action. (…) Revolutionary action is in every respect analogous to action as embodied in literature; the passage from nothing to everything, the affirmation of the absolute as event and of every event as absolute. (…) The writer sees himself in the Revolution. It attracts him because it is the time during which literature becomes history. It is his truth. Any writer who is not induced by the very fact of writing to think 'I am the revolution, only freedom allows me to write', is not really writing. (…) Literature contemplates itself in revolution, it finds its justification in revolution, and if it has been called the Reign of Terror, this is because its ideal is indeed that moment in history, that moment when 'life endures death and maintains itself in it' in order to gain from death the possibility of speaking and the truth of speech. (Blanchot 1995, 318-322)

The event of literature accomplishes in its free, excessive relationship between author and readers a break with the restricted economy of the project, with rational calculation and with the spirit of seriousness. It is "a break with the spirit of seriousness, expenditure, nihilation (…) liberation from the spirit of seriousness, the end of economies the overthrowing of hierarchies, and the absorption of the Other by the Same, of the objective by the subjective, of order by disorder." (Sartre 1992, 374) It opens up a common discourse through a certain apocalypse liberating author and reader (from themselves) by putting them on terrain "where they have to destroy themselves." (ibid., 375)

Is it then really surprising that the apocalypse of the literary event with its foundation of a new community re-emerges precisely in the revolutionary center of *Critique of Dialectical Reason*, that is, in those sections in which Sartre elaborates his presentation of the revolutionary collective: the fused group?[5]

Let us highlight briefly the evental character of the revolutionary fused group: The fused group, which is *not* and is an excess, emerges from a revolt against serial alienation, against the proliferation of alterity; as dissolution of capitalist bourgeois society, it is a resurrection of human freedom. Individual praxes are fused with other individual praxes in a kind of apocalypse of human revolt in order to burst open a new episode of true humanity in terms of freedom and reciprocity. Like the apocalypse of the literary work of art, the apocalypse of the revolutionary group praxis engenders humanity as a performative event, as the miracle of a *creatio ex nihilo*, that, in a sense, does not occur in time, but rather interrupts teleologies and causal chains – it is pure invention; it marks the possibility to transform impossibility into possibility. And the revolutionary group praxis implies the symbolic death of isolated subjects; it transforms them, in so far as they are no longer the same after the event of revolution; finally, the fused group also carries its justification in itself since it rejects normative criteria or the assignment of external apriori principles.

Truth

Badiou's truth is innovation *en acte*, always an intervention, always singular with respect to its site and its occasion, but universal and egalitarian regarding its address and its effect. Truth is always the truth of a situation; however, it does not concern those elements most identified, but rather the imperceptible groupings of elements. In short, the truth of a situation concerns always the generic; it is a generic grouping that occurs as break with the status quo. It makes claims to universality precisely as supplement to a concrete social situation that do not rely upon interest or privilege, but rather affirm the strictly generic universality of all members of a situation. In other words, Badiou's epistemological as well as practical-political notion of truth never re-affirms or stabilizes the privileged part of the situation, but its site is determined through the proximity to that which is the most anonymous in a situation: that is, what is, according to the logic of situation, "impossible."

---

[5] See the excellent passages on Sartre in Suzanne Guerlac's *Literary Polemics: Bataille, Sartre, Valery, Breton* (Guerlac 1997); I draw here on her illuminating remarks regarding the relationship of politics and aesthetics in Sartre.

Badiou's politics of truth is thus subjective and egalitarian-universal: subjectivity and universality do not mutually exclude each other, but are the two sides of the same coin. This committed truth-position is therefore an equation of the claim of universality with a militant, divisive position on the part of those subjects who participate in this struggle. Žižek reads Badiou's truth-process in terms of an identification of the universal with the point of exclusion, with the displaced element, and it is precisely here that he recognizes a correspondence with his own position. According to Žižek, proper politics always involves the gesture of universalization on the basis of a political agenda that cannot be realized within the existing system, and that puts it in question. "Politics proper thus always involves a kind of short circuit between the Universal and the Particular: the paradox of a *singulier universel*, a singular which appears as the stand-in for the Universal, destabilizing the 'natural' functional order of relations in the social body." (Žižek 2000, 188)

Even here one can discern several affinities to Sartre. According to Sartre, the event is a singular case that is located in the tensional field between singular and universal. If the event is singular, "it may not use explanations in terms of what is general except to demonstrate the presence of the general within the singular and as a singular form of the general." (Sartre 1992, 74-75) The singular universality of the event lapses neither into relativism nor into transcendent absolutism. Sartre writes that the event "never presents an absolute meaning that would be transcendent to the relative;" on the contrary, the event "is relative and the absolute is immanent within the relative." (ibid., 421) Moreover, Sartre emphasizes again and again that philosophy has to articulate the truth about man, but this philosophy can disclose itself only to revolutionaries, that is, to human beings who find themselves in the situation of being oppressed, and it needs them in order to manifest itself in the world. Sartre demonstrates that a split inhabits the true universal; his political gesture consists never simply in a protestation against the very injustice suffered by the oppressed or excluded in order to secure a public space in which their voices can be heard and recognized; rather, it represents them as stand-in for a claim to egalitarian universality disrupting the smooth circulation of negotiable particular interests, and it appears as a metaphorical condensation for the re-structuring of the social body: for the new invention of an egalitarian political space. Sartre's politics identifies the point of internal exclusion with the universal, thereby producing a kind of short circuit between the singular and the universal that, precisely as truth, stakes on the liquidation of alterity: "The truth in its original sense, therefore, as sociality and within an integrated group, is the elimination of all alterity." (Sartre 2004, 535) This short circuit between the singular and the universal that can be found in all three philosophers proves to be a politics that attempts to render possible the impossible. Sartre remarks: "The transformation therefore occurs when impossibility itself becomes possible, or when the synthetic event reveals that the impossibility of change is an impossibility of life." (ibid., 350) This also explains why this short circuit is not a mere subjective act of arbitrariness. That is, neither Sartre nor Žižek nor Badiou subscribe to a simple decisionism: the notion of a fully existential commitment is not reducible to a voluntarist leap, for it refers to a situation in which one no longer has alternatives or the possibility to take a step back in order to judge the situation from a distance; rather, full existential commitment recognizes that we are not free to decide or not to decide since the renunciation of decision would already constitute a (bad) decision.

As has been demonstrated convincingly by Thomas Flynn, one cannot think truth as universal in Sartre without a free, reciprocal, and egalitarian praxis; (Flynn 1996, 448-465)[6] ultimately, it is possible only in the egalitarian group that – another correspondence with Badiou – has generic equality as its epistemological and political axiom. This correspondence will be addressed in more detail in a moment.

Sartre then poses the question of a fidelity to the truth-process when he remarks that evidential truth has to be seen in a context with a pledge that keeps simulacra and epistemic alterity at a distance: "It is at this still practical level that the group has a silent knowledge of itself through each common individual: but this understanding (*évidence*) is not available to those who do not share its objectives." (Sartre 2004, 501) Fidelity to the truth-process will thus be the form of a fidelity to some pledge.

According to Badiou, the only true experience of fidelity is the result of an event. This fidelity to the truth-event is not something that could be described, but it rather amounts to something like a performative speech-act; this means that the effect of fidelity is, in a way, already operative on us before we even have arrived at fidelity. This is the reason why Badiou begins to distinguish between two moments of fidelity: the initial, primary fidelity to respond to the event as event; and the secondary fidelity whose task it is to remain faithful to the primary fidelity. Badiou writes: "But since the truth-process is fidelity, then if 'Do not give up' is the maxim of consistency – and thus of the ethic of truth – we might well say that it is a matter, for the 'some-one', of *being faithful to a fidelity*. (Badiou 2001, 47) While primary fidelity is experienced as disorder of our previous mode of being that suspends our certainties and dissolves our simulacra, one has to ask the question as to how one can remain faithful to this disorder. This constitutes the issue of secondary fidelity.

---

[6] Flynn's excellent essay shows in detail that truth and politics are conceptualized by the later Sartre as dissolution of alterity and as production of reciprocity and strict equality. What is more, truth in the egalitarian sense is possible solely in the free group; Sartre's politics is, as Flynn remarks, "vertically, the levelling of hierarchies and, horizontally, the realization of positive reciprocity."(Flynn 1996, 457-458)

If primary fidelity is identified as disorder or rupture, then secondary fidelity has to be grasped as the paradoxical attempt to organize something like consistency. The fidelity to fidelity implies the following question: "how will I, as some-one, *continue* to exceed my own being?" (Badiou 2001, 50) If we consider the revolutionary event in the light of Sartre's fused group, then primary fidelity marks that moment which leads to the apocalyptic formation of a group that can no longer be grasped in terms of a mere collection, gathering, or accumulation of individuals. This apocalyptic formation of a group via primary fidelity does, however, not suffice since the group must be maintained consistently precisely in its movement of permanent surpassing. That is, the group has to find a way to continue the very disorder that characterizes it. Fidelity is thus split between disorder and organization, break and preservation. And this reduplication of fidelity is rendered by Sartre in terms of the fused group and of the pledge as socialized praxis. Again, the fused group represents a break with seriality, it is the elimination of alterity, the suspension of opinions that, for Sartre as well as for Badiou, are nothing but "the cement of sociality (…) the primary material of all *communication*." (ibid., 50-51) This break – with an ethics of communication via an ethic of the Real (ibid., 52) – is presented as disorder, as "upheaval which destroys the collective by the flash of a common *praxis*" (Sartre 2004, 349) and, finally, as apocalypse, as abrupt resurrection of freedom that has as its primary moment of fidelity the "watchword," a unification without appeal to alienating orders. But it is exactly here that the issue of preserving the fused group becomes virulent: a "practical device" is needed in order to bind the group in unity and permanence – and this "practical device" is the pledge. This act of pledging can only be a common one: "the order is 'Let us swear'. This means that I also make myself, both in and for him (the Third), a guarantee that alterity cannot come to him through me." (ibid., 421) We will return below to this group characterized by "pledged fidelity."

Subject

If the subject (in Badiou and, perhaps, in Sartre's *Critique of Dialectical Reason*) is generated solely via the fidelity to truth, if it is an effect of the event and of the fidelity to the event, would one not have to call in question this account of subjectivity? In Žižek's words: "So (…) is not Badiou's notion of the Truth-Event uncannily close to Althusser's notion of (ideological) interpellation?" (Žižek 2000, 145) That is to say, is there, for Badiou, no subject outside of the truth-event, as there is for Althusser no subject outside of interpellation? Do subject and subjectivization coincide for Badiou (and Sartre)? For it seems that the commitment to the event induces retroactively a singular subject. This means, however, that the subject relies entirely and unconditionally on this commitment; that it is fully absorbed into this commitment, existing solely in the externality of an affirmation of truth. Moreover, Badiou seems to think that his conception of an empty, non-substantial, anti-psychological subject without a vis-à-vis is in agreement with Sartre's and Lacan's conceptions of the subject,[7] in so far as both think the subject via the question of decision: "The subject constitutes itself only where there is the place of decision, and each decision is, as true decision, ultimately a unique decision." (Badiou et al. 1997, 26, my transl.) But this claim of an alleged correspondence obscures, perhaps, fundamental differences. It is in the name of Lacan that Žižek insists that subject and the gesture of subjectivization have to be kept separate in a strict manner: subjectivization is the interpellation of the subject (or fidelity to the event), whereas the subject "is the negative gesture of breaking out of the constraints of Being that opens up the space of possible subjectivization." (Žižek 2000, 160)

Where is one, however, to really place Sartre's conception of the subject in this debate? Bosteels seems to suggest that Sartre's conception of the (committed) subject finds itself in a full correspondence with Badiou's engaged fidelity, with the embrace of the Cause versus a cause. (Bosteels 2005, 221-244, 237) But how could one reconcile this account of the Sartrean committed subject with Sartre's recourse to the Cartesian cogito and

---

[7] These claims are made by Peter Hallward in his excellent *Badiou: A Subject of Truth* (Hallward 2003, xviii). Hallward quotes also Badiou's statement that, due to the concept of the subject – a subject without a vis-a-vis – shared by Lacan, Sartre, and himself, a "re-grouping of Lacan, Sartre, and myself" would be possible. On page xxxi, Hallward returns to Badiou's appropriation of the Sartrean subject: he claims that this appropriation concerns mainly the subject of *Being and Nothingness*; he also mentions that Badiou subtracts from Sartre's freedom its ontological justification. This, however, leads precisely to the question whether Badiou does not reduce the subject to mere subjectivization (the subject as "secretion of Nothingness" remains underdetermined) – a question Hallward returns to toward the end of his study. His critical remarks revolve around the relation between true subject and "objective individual" (ibid., 279); however, he does not take recourse to Sartre. And even his question whether one finds in Badiou one subject or multiple subjects could be related to Sartre's incessant attempt to keep separate the subject as individual praxis and the group (as constituted dialectic). Anyway, Hallward presents a very fine summary of Badiou's reading of the *Critique of Dialectical Reason* (see ibid., 41-43).

From a different perspective, Bruno Bosteel's instructive essay "Badiou without Žižek," (Bosteel 2005, 221-244) takes issue with what he considers to be Žižek's highly appropriative and transcoding strategy of reading Badiou. Bosteel's essay is primarily an attempt to liberate Badiou's texts from the framework of Žižek's interpretation which, he claims, follows the (Lacanian) matrix of "x with y" whereby "y" reveals the truth of "x": an interpretation that, so Bosteels, has been able to exercise a hegemonic force on Anglo-American discussions of Badiou's work. Bosteels attempts to subtract Žižek from Badiou, primarily by bringing into play several central texts by Badiou that, according to Bosteels, have in many ways already anticipated and refuted Žižek's main critical points. For a critical rejoinder to Bosteels by Žižek see Slavoj Žižek, *The Parallax View* (Žižek 2006, 64).

to its capacity of abstracting itself from everything, of negating everything, of tearing itself away from the world? Would this, perhaps, suggest an even worse alternative: that of the Sartrean subject standing fully under the sign of an irreducible and constitutive lack, forever barred from the Cause or Thing? In other words, would Sartre's conception of the subject not find itself in a secret complicity with merely "idealist" problems of desire, its constitutive lack, and so on? Or is it not, rather, the case that Sartre's being-for-itself is not sufficiently accounted for by this idealist framework? Recall that the being-for-itself is characterized not only in terms of its capacity to negate beings in the world, but, more fundamentally, in terms of its *original nihilation*: that is, Sartre's subject, similar to that of Žižek, is marked by a radical negativity that can bring about a transformation of the very coordinates conditioning its being-in-the-world – again, not only conditions *within* its being-in-the-world, but also the *very* conditions *of* its being-in-the-world. That is, Sartre insists that our "being-in-the-world" is already the result of an original choice. Both Žižek's Hegelian-Lacanian subject and Sartre's "existentialist" subject are to be grasped in terms of self-relating negativity, withdrawal-into-self, "night of the world," death drive (Žižek), or as original nihilation, violent upsurge (Sartre), and they emerge as fissures in the texture of being that cannot be filled up by any subjectivization, thus testifying to the destitution that, ultimately, *is* the subject. Finally, both conceptions of the subject seem to share constant (simultaneous) associations of subject with the abject, with the excremental on the one hand, and (revolutionary) liberating violence on the other hand: a violence by means of which the subject seems to liberate itself from all empirical features, reduces itself to a Nothingness, thereby putting to risk (and annihilating) its symbolic identity. This radical subject in the act, the act of annihilation, is revolutionary precisely through its violence. Sartre writes: "this irrepressible violence (…) is man recreating himself." (Sartre 1963, 21) Revolutionary emancipatory freedom is, for Žižek, directly identifiable with violence: "it is violence as such (the violent gesture of discarding, of establishing a difference, of drawing a line of separation) which liberates. Freedom is not a blissfully neutral state of harmony and balance, but the very violent act which disturbs the balance." (Žižek 2003, 33) And Sartre seconds with his account of the upsurge of the revolutionary group: "The fact that the origin of the grouping was Terror is not actually very significant; every *praxis* constitutes itself as an opening made in the future, and sovereignly affirms its own possibility (…) As the freedom of revolt reconstitutes itself as common violence (…), its future objectification becomes, for it, the free violence of men against misery and impossibility of living." (Sartre

2004, 405) We find thus in both Žižek and Sartre an ontology of the subject as essentially revolutionary subject: a revolutionary subject that is inherently marked by pure violence.[8]

Militant Community

According to Sartre, the revolutionary group posits itself as the free medium of free human realizations. On the basis of the pledge it produces man as free common individual, rendering possible for the other his/her re-birth; the revolutionary group is the absolute end as pure freedom liberating men from alterity. As Sartre states more precisely: the pledge "is the origin of humanity." (Sartre 2004, 436) Furthermore: "This beginning therefore directs recognition to the reciprocal affirmation of these two *common* characteristics: we are *the same* because we emerged from the clay at the same date, through each other and through all others. (...) In other words, *our common being* is not *an identical nature* in everyone." (ibid., 437) It is through the pledge that the group becomes a mediated reciprocity (of conditionings); each praxis becomes the same as every other. The group enters the milieu of the same. It is here that one finds the birth of fraternity, the universal equality of everybody in relation to everybody else: the singular praxes conquer universal sameness by transforming their alterity. "in approaching a third party, I do not recognise my inert essence as mani-

---

[8] The issue of violence and terror is complex in both Sartre and Žižek. While Badiou addresses the problem of terror (in *On Metapolitics*) in the context of the "Thermidorean operation" – he points out that "the attempt to ‚think terror' is impractical as such, because the isolation of the category of terror is precisely a Thermidorean operation (...). It is an operation designed to produce something unintelligible and unthinkable. Considered in isolation, terror becomes an infra-political datum, one that is politically unthinkable, thereby leaving the terrain wide open for moralistic preaching against acts of violence" (Badiou 2005, 138) – and insists on the revolutionary work as a homogeneous multitude from which terror cannot be separated (that is why terror is a political problem and not simply a barbaric evil or crime), Sartre and Žižek emphasize the certainty of violence and even terror much stronger in terms of ontological implications of the subject of revolution. I have already indicated that the conception of pure expenditure and excess plays a prominent role in the Sartrean event of literature and of politics. It is before this background that one would have to re-examine Hannah Arendt's claim (in *On Violence*) that violence in Sartre is to be grasped in instrumental terms, for both Žižek as well as Sartre attempt to discern different registers of violence. And in both cases, "pure violence" – a violence that exhibits a certain affinity to Walter Benjamin's "actual state of exception" in opposition to the state of exception that aims merely at maintaining existing law and order – is taken to be as a signpost of "authentic revolutionary explosion." For Sartre, see, above all, his preface to Frantz Fanon's *Wretched of the Earth* and his writings on colonialism (as well as the passages on the revolutionary group in *Critique of Dialectical Reason*); for Žižek, see his *Iraq: The Borrowed Kettle* (Žižek 2004, 158-159), and see also his *The Parallax View* (Žižek, 2006, 380-381). See above all Neil Roberts' "Sartre, Fanon, Violence, and Freedom" (Roberts, 2004, 139-160). This essay is instrumental to my claim that Sartre's notion of violence must not be reduced to an instrumentalist understanding

fested in some other instance; instead I recognise my necessary accomplice in the act which removes *us* from the soil: my brother, whose existence *is not other than mine* approaches me as my existence and yet depends on mine as mine depends on his..."(ibid., 405) On account of the "creative act of the pledge" we "have become brothers," and our particular identities have become insignificant. Sartre continues: "(…) we *are our own sons,* our common creation." (ibid., 405) And: "The constituted group is produced in and by everyone as *his birth as a common individual* and, at the same time, everyone can grasp, in fraternity, his own birth as a common individual as having been produced in and by the group." (ibid., 438) Consequently the group is the product of the work of a community of common individuals (of Badiou's *some-ones*). The relation of individual praxis and group mirrors dialectically the relationship of cause and effect. On the one hand, the cause (of the group) is without doubt the product of the activity of individual praxes; it is alive only, in so far as it is continuously renewed by the passion of individual praxes. On the other hand, these individual praxes experience the cause (of the group) as the absolute that sets them in motion: that is, as cause of their activity. Individual praxes posit the cause (of the group), but they do not posit it as something that is subordinate, but rather as their absolute cause.

It has already been mentioned that the subjects undergo at this point a symbolic death, that is, they lose their symbolic identity: their predicative particularisms are suspended, and they re-emerge as common individuals. That is, what is lost in this transubstantiation is precisely the (particular) substance, that which the (bourgeois) subject considers the most precious kernel of his individuality. And Sartre does not hide that fact that this transubstantiation, by means of which the particular selfhood of the individual dies, is a horrifying, violent, and traumatic process, perhaps similar to the ubiquitous motif in science fiction of changed identity (for example, one could refer here the numerous passages in which Sartre renders in graphic details the very violence and trauma necessarily involved in the attempt of the colonized to bring about their own re-birth outside of the matrix of colonialism; incidentally, Sartre implies on more than one occasion that a successful and total liberation would also have to address the very link that keeps the oppressed bound to the system of oppression; that is, Sartre suggests, not unlike Žižek, that the colonized has to strike not only against the colonizer, but also, in a way, against herself or himself: against her or his attachment to the colonial system. Therein lies, for Sartre, the great significance of the work of Frantz Fanon; and as Žižek has remarked ironically, it is therefore no wonder that current multiculturalist, "radical" post-colonial theory has been characterized by the remarkable and convenient absence (and exclusion) of Fanon's thought and its refusal to subsume the struggle against colonialism, exploitation, and oppression simply under some discourse of victimization, of identity politics, and of the right to recognition).

Annihilation – conversion – re-birth: does this sequence of the Sartrean group whose thinking produces sameness out of alterity by remaining indifferent to differences, not anticipate the very militant community that, for Badiou as well, is organized around "the Real of a radical fraternity?" After all, Badiou states with regard to the possibility of a strictly egalitarian community: "Only that which will present itself *as a discourse of the Son* has the potential to be universal, detached from every particularism." (Badiou 2003, 43) And: "It is quite true that all postevental universality equalizes sons through the dissipation of the particularity of the fathers." (ibid., 59) This dissipation is, however, not simply an abolition of particularity; the task is rather, as Badiou elaborates with regard to Paul and the question of Jewish particularity, to animate Jewish particularity "internally by everything of which it is capable relative to the new discourse, and hence the new subject." (ibid., 103) And it is precisely this strategy of "subsequent symmetrization"(ibid., 104) – identified by Badiou in Saint Paul – that one finds repeatedly in Sartre. Just one example: In *Anti-Semite and Jew*, Sartre conceives the "authentic French Jew" as the very place of the singular universal, as singular universality and power of negativity subverting the fixations or "reifications" of particularism in French society. (See Vogt 2003, 123) And precisely this Sartrean politics of authenticity with its sole maxim of not giving up on one's own split (as singular universal) is evoked by Badiou in the following passage:

> With regard to what has happened to us (…) differences are indifferent, and the universality of the true collapses them. With regard to the world in which truth proceeds, universality must expose itself to all differences and show, through the ordeal of their division, that they are capable of welcoming the truth that traverses them. What matters, man or woman, Jew or Greek, slave or free man, is that differences *carry the universal that happens to them like a grace*. Inversely, only by recognizing in differences their capacity for carrying the universal that comes upon them can the universal itself verify its own reality. (Badiou 2003, 106)[9]

---

[9] In *Politics of Friendship*, Jacques Derrida comments on "the gravest problem" of fraternity or fraternization: "Of course, no one will contest the fact that all movements (Christian or revolutionary ones, for example) celebrating fraternity or fraternal friendships have universal range and theoretically challenge the limits of natural, literal, genetic, sexually determined (etc.) fraternity."(Derrida 1997, 237) But why then Derrida's reticence about the discourse of fraternity? "In keeping this word to designate a fraternity beyond fraternity, a fraternity without fraternity (literal, strict, masculine, etc.), one never renounces that which one claims to renounce – and which returns in myriad ways, through symptoms and disavowals whose rhetoric we must learn to decipher and whose strategy to outwit." (ibid.) It is, perhaps, Badiou's and Sartre's "subsequent symmetrization" that accomplishes the very outwitting that, to a certain extent, Derrida wants to preserve in Blanchot when he remarks: "What can the name ‚brother' or the call to fraternity still mean when one or the other arises in the speech of friendship which, like that of Blanchot […] has so radically delivered itself from the hold of all de-

Badiou's egalitarian, universal, and revolutionary collective of sons is thus elaborated in the context of a reading of Saint Paul. Fully subscribing to Badiou's appropriation of Pauline universalism, Žižek comments:

> The Christian community (…) designates a new collective held together not by a Master-Signifier, but by a fidelity to a Cause, by the effort to draw a new line of separation that runs 'beyond Good and Evil', that is to say, that runs across and suspends the distinctions of the existing social body. The key dimension of Paul's gesture is thus his break with any form of communitarianism: his universe is no longer that of the multitude of groups that want to 'find their voice,' and assert their particular identity, their 'way of life,' but that of a fighting collective grounded in the reference to an unconditional universalism. (Žižek 2003, 130)

Could this, finally, mean that, in addition to "the revolutionary party and the psychoanalytic society" as "further examples of this same collective," (ibid.)[10] one would have to include as well the Sartrean group as a another version of Pauline-Christian universalism?

Prof. Dr. Erik M. Vogt, Trinity College, Hartford, erik.vogt(at)trincoll.edu

References

Badiou, Alain, Jacques Rançiere, Rado Riha, *Politik der Wahrheit*, Vienna: Turia + Kant, 1997.
Badiou, Alain. *Ethics: An Essay on the Understanding of Evil*. Translated and introduced by Peter Hallward, London, New York: Verso, 2001.

---

termined communities, all filiation or affiliation – families or peoples – or even all given generality…?" (ibid., 304)

[10] Here, one would have to examine, above all, the simultaneity of revolutionary (redemptive) violence and love. Badiou and Žižek repeatedly describe the Pauline community in terms of the work of love, and this work is the figure of revolutionary politics. One finds this simultaneity also in Sartre: in the *Critique of Dialectical Reason* he remarks that this violence (of the revolutionary group) "is the very power of this lateral reciprocity of love." (Žižek 2003, 439) Why this recourse to revolutionary collectives clearly inspired by Christian universalism? Perhaps because other conceptions of community – above all those in the context of neo-Heideggerianism – are characterized by a certain political impotence. Derrida's "New International" remains, beyond its affirmation of a democracy to come, politically empty. True, it is important to demonstrate the traditional identificatory notions of community in terms of collective identity in order to render possible a different perspective on community and on the processes of socialization. But is this endeavor really exhausted by the claim of an essential community "of those who have nothing in common," or by hypostatizing philosophically certain writers' organizations (such as PEN)? The suspicion remains that a certain asceticism regarding praxis and a certain dictate of pure politics (that without "dirty hands"; that of "beautiful souls") attempt to obscure current attempts (however imperfect and problematic) at collective action.

Badiou, Alain. *Saint Paul: The Foundation of Universalism*. Translated by Ray Brassier, Stanford: Stanford University Press, 2003.

Badiou, Alain. *Ethik.* Translated by Jürgen Brankel, Vienna: Turia + Kant, 2003a.

Badiou, Alain. *On Metapolitics*. Translated and with an Introduction by Jason Barker, London, New York: Verso, 2005.

Baugh, Bruce. "Sartre, Derrida, and Commitment: The Case of Algeria," *Sartre Studies International* 9.2 (December 2003), 16-40.

Blanchot, Maurice. *The Work of Fire*. Translated by Charlotte Mandell, Stanford: Stanford University Press, 1995.

Bosteels, Bruno. „Badiou without Žižek," *Polygraph* 17 (2005), 221 – 244.

Derrida, Jacques. *Politics of Friendship*. Translated by George Collins, London, New York: Verso, 1997.

Guerlac, Suzanne. *Literary Polemics: Bataille, Sartre, Valery, Breton*, Stanford: Stanford University Press, 1997.

Flynn, Thomas R. „An End to Authority: Epistemology and Politics in the Later Sartre," in William McBride (ed.). *Existentialist Politics and Political Theory*, New York: Garland Publishing, 1996, 448 – 465.

Hallward, Peter. *Badiou: A Subject of Truth*, Minneapolis, London: University of Minnesota Press, 2003.

Jameson, Fredric. *Marxism and Form*, Princeton: Princeton University Press, 1971.

Kesel, Marc de. „Truth as Formal Catholicism. On Alain Badiou, *Saint Paul. La Fondation de L'Universalisme*," in *Miracles Do Happen: Essays on Alain Badiou*, ed. Dominiek Hoens, Communication & Cognition, vol. 37, n. 3/4, 2004, 167 – 197.

Lévy, Bernard-Henri. *Sartre: The Philosopher of the Twentieth Century*. Translated by Andrew Brown, Cambridge, UK: Polity Press, 2003.

Rançiere, Jacques. *Disagreement: Politics and Philosophy*. Translated by Julie Rose, Minneapolis: University of Minnesota Press, 1998.

Roberts, Neil. "Sartre, Fanon, Violence, and Freedom," *Sartre Studies International*, vol. 10, no. 2, 2004, 139 – 160.

Sartre, Jean-Paul. *Anti-Semite and Jew*. Translated by George J. Becker (New York. Schocken Books, 1948.

Sartre, Jean-Paul. „Preface" to Frantz Fanon, *Wretched of the Earth*. Translated by Colin Farrington (New York: Grove Press, 1963), 21.

Sartre, Jean-Paul. *What is Literature? and Other Essays*. Translated by Bernard Frechtman, Jeffrey Mehlman, John MacCombie (Cambridge: Harvard University Press, 1988), 54.

Sartre, Jean-Paul. *Notebooks for an Ethics*. Translated by David Pellauer (Chicago: University of Chicago Press, 1992), 35.

Sartre, Jean-Paul. *Critique of Dialectical Reason: Volume 1*. Translated by Alan Sheridan-Smith; ed. by Jonathan Rée; foreword by Fredric Jameson, London, New York: Verso, 2004.

Vogt, Erik M. *Sartres Wieder-holung*, Vienna: Passagen Verlag, 1995.

Vogt, Erik M. *Zugänge zur politischen Ästhetik*, Vienna: Turia + Kant, 2003.

Žižek, Slavoj. *The Ticklish Subject: the absent centre of political ontology*, London, New York: Verso, 2000.

Žižek, Slavoj. *The Puppet and the Dwarf: The Perverse Core of Christianity*, Cambridge, London: MIT Press, 2003.

Žižek, Slavoj. *Iraq: The Borrowed Kettle*, London, New York: Verso, 2004.

Žižek, Slavoj. *The Parallax View*, Cambridge, London: MIT Press, 2006.

PETER KAMPITS (Vienna)

The Actuality of Sartre's Free Will Conception

Abstract

The main Sartrean concepts and theses of freedom of will and unlimited responsibility, which seemed for many already outdated, are gaining actually interest in respect to the recent results in brain research. The main objective of the paper is to reevaluate Sartre's free will conception trying to answer the question: How would Sartre who, in the time of his existentialist phase during which his radical theory of freedom received its most pointed articulation, was familiar with psychological theories of determinism, have responded to statements of actually leading brain researchers such as "we are determined," "brain research liberates from illusions" or "I am my brain"?

Keywords: Jean-Paul Sartre, freedom, will, determinism, brain research, otherness, ontology, ethics

---

Although Sartre's theses on freedom as the very being of man and, consequently, on a near unlimited responsibility had encountered fierce resistance already more than fifty years ago, this situation has intensified because of the most recent results and theses in brain research. For brain research claims that freedom is an illusion. It is not I who is thinking, but rather my brain plays a game of neurons, and our selves are as much an illusion as our freedom.

Of course, these claims have provoked opposition by philosophers who oppose to this specter of determinism category mistakes (naturalist fallacy; hermeneutic naïvité), and who attempt to salvage human freedom by means of notions of the life-world. Or they speak, as most recently John Searle, of the experience of a gap located between causes preceding of our decisions and the execution of our actions. Even sharper is the opposition on the side of lawyers, in so far as the denial of free decisions challenges decisively ethics and existing law.

How would Sartre who, in the time of his existentialist phase during which his radical theory of freedom received its most pointed articulation, was familiar with psychological theories of determinism, have responded to statements of leading brain researchers such as "we are determined," "brain research liberates from illusions" or "I am my brain"?

It would of course be easy to completely separate Sartre's theory of freedom which is elaborated at an ontological level from the debate about determinism. However, Sartre dealt extensively with the problems of will, of freedom of choice, and of – psychological – determinism, and he attempted, within the framework of his thesis that there is freedom only in situation and situation only through freedom – the facticity of freedom -, to refute possible objections.

At first glance, Sartre's thesis that freedom and being human coincide appears indeed radical, even absolutist. It is clear for Sartre that freedom, considered at an ontological level, is not a quality, not a capacity of man, not a matter of will, but rather a mode of being: "Human freedom precedes essence in man and makes it possible; the essence of the human being is suspended in his freedom. (...) Man does not exist *first* in order to be free *subsequently*; there is no difference between the being of man and his *being-free*." (Sartre 1984, 60)

Sartres ontological position derives this freedom from the structure of nihilation characterizing human existence, that is, of the being-for-itself that, for Sartre, is defined as a being "which is not what it is and which is what it is not." (ibid., 127)

This seemingly paradoxical claim depends on the fundamental ontological distinction marking Sartre's *Being and Nothingsness*: that between being-in-itself (*être-en-soi*) and being-for-itself (*être-pour-soi*). Sartre's point of departure is that, ontologically speaking, consciousness and the very phenomenon encountered by consciousness represent ultimately two heterogeneous, although mutually related forms of being. The structure of intentionality that, taken over from Husserl, fundamentally informs consciousness, is, so to speak, ontologized by Sartre. While, in Sartres's precise diction, beings of the mode of being of the being-in-itself are to be grasped as mere positivity and identity, without any otherness, the being-for-itself has to be regarded as something that always already includes a reference to something other than itself, that can never be identical with itself.

Here, Sartre provides essentially two arguments. The phenomenological argument has to do with the intentional structure of consciousness: there is no substantial inhabitant of consciousness (no empirical or transcendental Ego), but rather a being-directed of consciousness toward something other than itself. This is to be demonstrated by the pre-reflective cogito. At the same time, the structure of consciousness is ontologized at a second level. Since consciousness is always consciousness of something, it is always directed at something that is, precisely, not itself. It always has to "be outside of itself." This structure of intentionality leads not only to the insight that man cannot be determined by an essence or something like a human nature preceding him, but also to the recognition that man is first defined solely by means of his existence; reversing traditional ontological categories, one has to claim that his existence precedes his essence: "Consciousness is a being whose existence posits its essence." (ibid., 24) In other words: "*consciousness is a being such that in its being, its being is in question in so far as this being implies a being other than itself.*" (ibid.)

At the same time, an ontological act is required in order to ground this difference, that is, an act through which nothingness enters the being-for-itself; for it is this "Nothingness," this "hole in being," this fall of the in-itself into the itself, through which the for-itself is constituted, finds its central ontological definition: "The Being by which Nothingness arrives in the world is a being such that in its Being, the Nothingness of its Being is in question. *The being by which Nothingness comes to the world must be its own Nothingness.*" (ibid., 58-59) Man, "*la realité humaine*," as Sartre calls this, is characterized in such a way that, in its being, a being is included that it is not itself. Man is never identical with himself (he is presence to self); he is always separated from himself, that is, he has to be and is not because he is not what he is. And this is, for Sartre, the very foundation of freedom: the possibility to create Nothingness out of oneself.

This condensed reminder of the fundamental ontological structure of human reality can form the basis for Sartre's further reflections on freedom.

One has to bear in mind that the radicality with which Sartre posits this notion of freedom emerges from the ontological basic structure rendering comprehensible formulations like the one mentioned at the beginning: "We are condemned to freedom"; "man cannot be sometimes slave and sometimes free; he is wholly and forever free or he is not free at all." (ibid., 569)

It is well-known that Sartre defended this ontologically grounded conception against many objections: objections coming from determinism, from common sense, and from the metaphysical tradition. It is interesting that Sartre claims the need for a theory of action as necessary basis for a discussion of determinism by pointing to the need for the being-for-itself to do, instead of simply to be. He proceeds again from the idea of the intentionality of consciousness in order to demonstrate that nihilation is an essential part in the positing of the end of action. The "tedious discussions between determinists and the proponents of free will" miss the real issue. (ibid., 563) The failure of this debate (concerning here, however, psychological determinists) is that the chain "motive – intention – action – end" is not undermined. For the causal chain – affirmed by the determinists and remaining indifferent for the non-determinists – has to be replaced by a model of intentionality in which the act, the choice, decides itself the motives.

Unlike the debate regarding the results of brain research, in which advocates of freedom often advance the distinction between reasons and causes – "brains react on the basis of causes, human beings act on the basis of reasons" -, Sartre does not mention this distinction. The response given by brain researchers shows how little this distinction can contribute to the issue of freedom: for, as Gerhard Roth argues, reasons would then be the conscious form of experiencing brain processes, the "internal" lived aspect, while *causes* would be the "external, neurophysiological aspect" of those processes. (Roth 2004, 66-85, 82) Of course, here one could raise many objections; however one could at least debate, whether the old idealist-metaphysical distinction between an empirical and a transcendental level is really sufficient, especially since Kant's distinction between a causality of nature and a causality from freedom re-opens that dualism which, as *tema con variazioni*, has permeated the history of philosophy, for instance, in form of the body-soul problem.

Without being able to go through the whole spectrum of arguments and counter-arguments regarding freedom, what is essential is that they bear, essentially, similar metaphysical imprints; thus, they operate at a level that is fundamentally different from Sartre's conception of freedom and of human reality.

For Sartre, the whole issue of free will is at bottom obsolete. If one takes as one's point of departure his almost circular model of action in which the act or choice itself decides the motives, then the intentionality of the structure of consciousness is the decisive factor for my choice and my decision: "It is the act which decides its ends and its motives, and the act is the expression of freedom." (Sartre 1984, 127)

Sartre's argument lies here in the double aim of action. In intentionality, the being-directed towards an end reveals itself as world, and at the same time this defines my possibility as choice.

Moreover, the issue of free will is too reductionist for Sartre. According to him, the will as a kind of conscious state represents an idol of positive psychology; it presupposes the foundation of an original freedom in order to be able to constitute itself as will. (ibid., 571)

For the will does not create any ends; it defines itself via these ends since the human being, so Sartre, cannot receive ends: it cannot receive "external" or "internal" ones. Although Sartre does not define them in more detail, one can designate them with reference to brain research as those that are determined by physiological and neuronal brain processes. Due to the nihilating structure of the being-for-itself freedom remains the foundation of the very ends that I attempt to accomplish. Thus, Sartre draws the provocative conclusion that the will is determined in a transcendent project of itself towards its possibilities within the framework of motives and goals. (ibid.)

It is from this perspective that Sartre analyses the complex of motive and reasons. He is fundamentally convinced that the project of action remains decisive for *mobiles, motives, fins*: They all refer back to the relation between consciousness and the world. What is decisive for Sartre is that a voluntary deliberation is always a deception. It is worth pursuing his argument in detail: causes and motives receive their significance only via choice. They are not "transcendent things," they receive their weight only through my free project. Thus Sartre can claim: "When I deliberate, the chips are down." (ibid., 581)

Moreover: "When the will intervenes, the decision is taken, and it has no other value than that of making the announcement." (ibid.)

Surprisingly, this ontological foundation of the will going back to the fundamental structure of the being-for-itself corresponds to the arguments by brain researchers: decisions and actions are prepared by neuronal processes and are ultimately decided by the brain. When the will appears, everything is already decided.

Sartre provides an impressive example that undermines common *doxa*, according to which being free means that a choice could have been otherwise. He mentions here the situation of a human being who is on a hiking trip with other friends. If I am overwhelmed by fatigue and refuse to continue walking, I can be admonished to get my act together and walk with the others to the next resting place. Sartre claims that the possibility to overcome my fatigue or to give in to it obscures the real issue: for the real issue is that I cannot act otherwise without changing my entire being-in-the-world. This means, however, that I am referred back to the original nihilation that constitutes the being-in-the-world of being-for-itself. And precisely this nihilation renders it impossible to proceed from something given, factual. According to Sartre, this is already ruled out by the structure of intentionality that cannot be explained by means of a given. Rather, the act is a break with the given, a break that, at the same time, causes this given: that is, it causes that this given is revealed in the light of that which is not yet.

Certainly, Sartre's elaborations do not refer here to the interplay of brain and consciousness; however, the fundamental structure of intentionality with its nihilating character is then further elaborated in the context of freedom and facticity of situation. The main task is here to defend the notion of freedom against a series of objections. The "enemy" is a certain common sense or a notion of freedom that conceives freedom as mental or internal freedom. Let us recall the following statement: "there is freedom only in a *situation*, and there is a situation only through freedom." (ibid., 629)

With this, the interplay of freedom and alleged limits of freedom are elevated to a different level. The seemingly determining givenness is revealed only through our choice, and our ends as possible limitations of our freedom:

> Far from being able to modify our situation at our whim, we seem to be unable to change ourselves. I am not 'free' either to escape the lot of my class, of my nation, of my family, or even to build up my own power or my fortune or to conquer my most significant appetites or habits. I am born a worker, a Frenchman, a hereditary syphilitic, or a tubercular. The history of a life, whatever it may be, is the history of a failure. (...) Much more than he appears 'to make himself', man seems 'to be made' by climate and the earth, race and class, language, the history of the collectivity of which he is a part, heredity, the individual circumstances of his childhood, acquired habits, the small and great events of his life. (ibid)

For Sartre, these do not constitute any objections against freedom; due to intentionality and its nihilating character, we never encounter a brute fact, but rather always already a given interpreted in the light of our free projects. In other words: "Thus freedom can be truly free only by constituting facticity as its own restriction." (ibid., 636) Sartre attempts to illustrate this via the reference to certain phenomena such as my place, my past, my environment, my death and, finally, my fellowman.

This attempt succeeds relatively well and convincingly regarding the first phenomena. Obstacles and adversities, as they emerge through my place (which is, by and large, for Sartre, the spatial facticity of my existence assigned to me by the contingency of my birth) do not restrict freedom at all. But this can be revealed only through the end posited by my freedom. Thus, my place is defined as obstacle or as spring-board. According to Sartre, this is further proof for the "inextricable connection of freedom and facticity in the situation." (ibid.) Something similar applies to my environment (*mes environs*) that Sartre conceives as the coefficients of adversity and of *Zeug* on the side of things that, due to the place, form my respective environment. Not even they – from the obstacle of a mountain that I cannot climb to accidents preventing me from achieving my goal – do represent restrictions of my freedom.

Sartre argues in a similar manner regarding the past. On the one hand, the past is facticity, that is, it is, in a way, unalterable; however, it receives its meaning only from the future towards which I project myself. Just as freedom is the choice of an end via a dependence on the past, the past is only that which it is regarding the chosen end. No more than the meaning of previous dates can be changed by me arbitrarily, the past can receive its meaning only in the light of a project directed towards the future. The future decides whether the past is alive or dead; "human reality" has a "*memorial* past *in suspense*." (ibid., 643) Historization of the being-for-itself is a perpetual affirmation of its freedom. The past exists, but it exists in terms of a being that I no longer am, but rather have to be.

The argument regarding the being-for-others that is, for Sartre, a decisive dimension of being-for-itself is, however, more difficult. The problematic of the relation to the other which is interlocked with the dimension of our embodiment that, in the context of the question concerning the interplay of brain and freedom, plays a special role, is of course a principal item of the ontological investigations in *Being and Nothingness*.

It is no coincidence that Sartre's analyses proceed from phenomena such as shame or look: that is, from phenomena of our embodiment. Being-looked-at, being ashamed are not only phenomena of embodiment, but they also reveal that the being-for-itself has constituted itself towards a new type of being: being-for-others. The highly detailed and convoluted analyses that Sartre devotes to being-for-others cannot be reconstructed here in full detail. (see Kampits 1975)

Sartre depicts the phenomena which the being-for-itself encounters in being-looked-at in a drastic manner: The look of the other objectifies me, it transcends my transcendence, it makes me part of the world and deprives me of my possibilities – and, finally, it alienates me from my freedom by petrifying me in my projects. But this story about my relation to the other has, of course, another side: for I have the possibility to objectify the other, to petrify his possibility, to alienate him from his freedom. Fundamentally, Sartre repeats the interplay of negation and project also at the level of the relation to the other, which means recognition of the other as well as his negation. I have to tear myself away from the other in a movement that is simultaneously recognition of the other and his negation. Precisely this negation means, however, at once negation and positing of the other: tearing myself away from and negating that which the other has reduced me to gives rise to the existence of the other. I recognize the other by negating and denying my Ego that has been attributed to me by him.

Put more graphically and simpler: The Ego that constantly eludes me because of the structure of freedom and consciousness is objectified and fixed by the other. At the same time, I tear myself away from this objectified Ego, I reject my Ego, and I determine myself in the very rejection of my Ego. Thus the conflict with the other is inevitable: my self-realization requires both the recognition and the annihilation of the other, the other that I must find in my inmost depths "as not being me." (Sartre 1984, 338)

At the same time, I experience myself as being thrown into the freedom of the other – and now I can either deny the very being attributed to me by the other by objectifying the other, or take hold of his freedom and transcendence without taking away its transcendent character. (ibid., 473-474)

The concrete relations to the other that Sartre sketches (love; language; masochism; indifference; desire; hatred; sadism) illustrate eloquently the mutual story of these relations. However, nowhere is the freedom of the other actually attained and recognized. It is either appropriated as freedom – and loses its character of freedom – or it remains freedom, unattainable for me in all eternity; thus the being-for-itself is constantly exposed to the risk of losing its own freedom.

Sartre pays special attention to the problem of the other as a possible restriction of my freedom, and what is central to his analyses is a world that is already populated by the other, already marked by meanings and givens. We exist in the world in the presence of others. Can this mean, especially with regard to the explication of the ontological structure of being-for-others, a restriction of my freedom? Sartre's answer can be told at once. Of course, the existence of the other posits a factual limit for my freedom. I experience myself as something that I have not chosen to be; I encounter a mode of being that I have not chosen. Ultimately, this is no restriction of my freedom, for I can grasp the other - and that which happens to me because of him – only in light of my own freedom. According to Sartre, this means "that my freedom by freely choosing itself chooses its limits." (ibid., 678)

It is for this reason that the freedom of the other cannot be a restriction of my freedom. That is, it can never encounter these limits, it can never realize them.

This fundamental position remains authoritative also for Sartre's investigations regarding embodiment. Roughly speaking, the very body that is of interest to physiologists and brain researchers cannot be designated "my body," but rather "body for others." For according to Sartre, the body as it is accessible to the surgeon or brain researcher is "*in the midst of the world* and as it is for others." (ibid., 402)

The resulting problems of the dualism of consciousness and body, of body and soul, characteristic of the entire philosophical tradition are resolved, as soon as the body is for me not experienced and comprehended as an external body-thing, but rather as lived body (*corps vécu*).

The body as body for me is part of the structure of the being of consciousness; it cannot be perceived as object, similar to the impossibility of seeing my own seeing. I do not have my body, as I have and possess certain things, but rather I am my body. It is for this very reason that the problem of brain researchers does not exist for Sartre: without denying that I "have," of course, a brain, a lung, a liver etc., the body remains thoroughly psychical: "First of all, it is evident that consciousness can exist its body only as consciousness. Therefore *my* body is a conscious structure of my consciousness." (ibid., 434)

While I am incapable of assuming an objectifying viewpoint regarding my own body, I can do so regarding the body as it appears for others. However, even the body of the other is not merely – and certainly not primordially – the body of physiology or anatomy, but rather "the facticity of the transcendence-transcended." (ibid., 457)

The mere body-thing would be, for Sartre, the corpse, that form of the body that becomes clear also in my being-for-others and its implied form of freedom: for Sartre, being dead means "to be a prey for the living." (ibid., 695) For death transforms us as a contingent fact into some "outside," ultimately into a "thing in the world," construed by the other, that is: into an in-itself. For this reason, there is no place for death within the being-for-itself. Sartre's attempt at fending off even death as a possible limitation of the freedom of the being-for-itself may not be entirely convincing or consistent in itself; his thesis regarding freedom is, however, as terse as debatable: like birth, death is a mere fact; it happens to us from outside, it transforms us into some outside; it has nothing to do with our finitude, it can neither be anticipated nor expected – even if we were immortal, we would remain finite being. We render ourselves finite by choosing ourselves: in freedom. Thus Sartre can claim regarding the structure of freedom of human existence that "our death is always *thrown into the bargain*." (ibid., 700)

What is essential to the question of the interplay of embodiment and freedom is, perhaps, not the so-called third dimension of our embodiment – that is, to exist for myself as body recognized by the other or, put simply, the consciousness of my body as it is for the other, or how it is alienated from me without, however, existing this alienation as final objectification -, but rather the very status that reveals to me this facticity through death. The corpse as "the *pure past of a life*, as simply the *remains*," (ibid., 402) presents itself as loss, as no longer in situation, as pure facticity. Sartre remarks ironically that not only anatomy, but also physiology finds here its starting point: Physiology appears as a synthetic reconstruction of the living person from the standpoint of corpses:

> From the outset physiology is condemned to understand nothing of life since it conceives life simply as a particular modality of death. (...) Even the study of life in the living person, even vivisection, even the study of protoplasm, even embryology or the study of the egg can not rediscover life; the organ which is observed is living but it is not established in the synthetic unity of *a particular* life; it is understood in terms of anatomy – i.e., in terms of death. (ibid., 457)

All these arguments make clear that human freedom cannot be affected by conditionalities of a physical or psychical nature. Sartre's ontological-existential argument is light years apart from that of brain researchers.

Yet, a certain parallel creeps in unexpectedly precisely in the context of the question of being-for-others. For the argument of brain researchers concedes something like a social context: in order to explain the "illusion of the self," educational and experiential processes are summoned stressing communicative, social-cultural influences based upon the symbolically oriented evolution of language. (Singer 2004, 52) Certainly, this is also designated as a condition enabling us to experience ourselves as autonomous, freely deciding beings. In other words: it is, according to Wolf Singer, "social interaction" (ibid., 49) that shows an ontological status that differs from that of the contents of the perception of the world of objects. Linguistic communication and so-called iterative processes of mirroring can account not only for our ability to distinguish between free and unfree decisions, but also for the fact that other human beings ascribe this freedom and responsibility to us already during early childhood.

This is reminiscent, albeit in a different dimension, of Sartre's being-for-others and of its situation of conflict that, however, does not relieve me of my responsibility. For being free means in this context a continuous conflict with the freedom of the other; it also means, however, that through this authorship one "carries the weight of the whole world on one's shoulders." (Sartre 1984, 402) Man, "condemned to be free (...) is responsible for the world and for himself as a way of being." (ibid., 707) In this sense, there is no destiny, neither because of my genes nor through a kind of social or historical situation, even if I am neither the ground of my being nor of the world, nor of the other. There are no excuses, not even those of certain structures of my brain and of neuronal processes: man "is no longer anything but a freedom which perfectly reveals itself and whose being resides in this very revelation." (ibid., 711)

It is the very question of responsibility that leads us far beyond the problematic of free will versus determination. Of course, Sartre demanded it with such force that the importance of free action seems almost exaggerated. Certainly, to tie responsibility back to one's own decision and choice renders it somewhat plausible, but can this responsibility – that, in the context of debates concerning brain research, contains not only implications for ethics, but also for law and, above all, criminal law – be expanded as far as Sartre demanded? Sartre charges not only the individual structure of freedom with this responsibility, in so far as the being-for-itself is the author of that into which it makes itself, and at the same time it is the one "by whom it happens that *there is* a world." (ibid., 707) With this – and this seems to be fully consistent – I have decided in the actions – the acts – of my freedom: "What happens to me happens through me" (ibid., 708) – however, can I expand this onto others? Here one encounters a shortcoming that, particularly with regard to the responsibility towards the other as problem, will push Sartre's thought into that social dimension that is also constitutive for brain research and its account of our assumption of freedom for social reasons, for reasons of assignment through the other.

> It seems that true freedom can only consist in a radical new beginning, in beginning again from anew – without any external constraints, but also independent of all needs, wishes and convictions that one usually attributes to oneself, but that are, in reality, only the products of dispositions and the environment. If one decides in such a situation for a particular option, then true freedom seems to assume that, under the very same conditions, one could have decided for a different option. (Pauen 2004, 8)

"Nobody can be different from who one is." (Singer 2004, 68) "Man is condemned to be free." (Sartre 2001, 32) One could ask the question whether there is an essential difference between these two statements, irrespective of the profound difference regarding the argumentative levels, the approaches, and the points of departure. Condemned to follow the neuronal play of my brain processes, or condemned to a freedom whose foundation I cannot be – do not both ultimately end up with more questions and challenges that put to the test anew the fragmentations of our life-world?

(Translated from German by Erik M. Vogt)

Prof. Dr. Peter Kampits, Vienna University, peter.kampits[at]univie.ac.at

Literaturangaben

Kampits, Peter. *Sartre und die Frage nach dem Anderen. Eine sozialontologische Untersuchung*. Wien, München: Oldenbourg, 1975.

Pauen, Michael. *Illusion Freiheit? Mögliche und unmögliche Konsequenzen der Hirnforschung*. Frankfurt am Main: Fischer, 2004.

Roth, Gerhard. "Worüber dürfen Hirnforscher reden – und in welcher Weise?," in Christian Geyer (ed.). *Hirnforschung und Willensfreiheit. Zur Deutung der neuesten Experimente*, Frankfurt am Main: Suhrkamp, 2004.

Sartre, Jean-Paul. *Being and Nothingness*.Translated and with an Introduction by Hazel E. Barnes. New York: Pocket Books, 1984.

Sartre, Jean-Paul. *Basic Writings*, ed. Stephen Priest. London and New York: Routledge, 2001.

Singer, Wolf. "Verschaltungen legen uns fest: Wir sollten aufhören, von Freiheit zu sprechen," in Christian Geyer (ed.). *Hirnforschung und Willensfreiheit. Zur Deutung der neuesten Experimente*, Frankfurt am Main: Suhrkamp, 2004, 30-65.

CONSTANCE L. MUI (New Orleans)
JULIEN S. MURPHY (Portland, Maine)

"Pierre Loves Horranges":
Sartre and Malabou on the Fantastic in Philosophy

Abstract

In "Pierre Loves Horranges ", a little noticed essay on Sartre's existential psychoanalysis, emerging French philosopher Catherine Malabou offers a new reading of "Doing and Having", in Sartre's Being and Nothingness for her philosophy of the fantastic. We compare Sartre and Malabou on the fantastic, focusing on their analyses of quality, viscosity and ontological difference. We argue that Malabou's reinterpretation of Sartre's symbolic schema, which serves to make visible the change and exchange in the ontological difference, is valuable for a psychoanalysis of the future, one that comes after metaphysics and deconstruction.

Key Words: Sartre, Malabou, ontology, psychoanalysis, plasticity, fantastic

Interest in Sartre's existential psychoanalysis has declined in recent years with one notable exception, Catherine Malabou, a rising voice in recent continental philosophy.[1] Sartre would no doubt be surprised at how few French women philosophers have garnered attention more than thirty-five years after his death. For instance, Ian James's recent collection, *The New French Philosophy,* includes only one woman, Catherine Malabou, while other recent French philosophy volumes turn up no other names (Badiou 2012; Gutting 2013, and Mullarkey 2006). Certainly, after Sartre's longstanding encouragement of Beauvoir – she credits him for the idea of *The Second Sex* – he would pause to learn that the related question of women's subjectivity and autonomy would remain unsettled as Malabou shows in *Changing Difference,* her work on feminist philosophy and essentialism. Malabou follows in the footsteps not of Irigaray, Kristeva, Cixous, or other French post-structuralist feminists, but of Derrida, who directed her thesis on Hegel. Derrida's influence could be

---

[1] We dedicate this paper to the memory of the one hundred thirty victims of the terrorist attacks in Paris on November 13, 2015.

seen throughout her work (Malabou, 2004). Malabou's philosophy is innovative in many respects, not the least of which is her concept of plasticity that she brings to her writings on psychoanalysis and neuroscience (Malabou 2009, Johnston and Malabou 2013).

Like the early Sartre, Malabou's writings, such as the *Ontology of the Accident*, are deeply engaged with Heidegger and the question of existence. Given the major influence of Heidegger and Hegel on *Being and Nothingness,* the young Sartre's treatise on ontology, it is curious to find only a few traces of Sartre in Malabou's published work. She cites Sartre in her book on Heidegger that appeared in 2004, and later in *Plasticity at the Dusk of Writing* (2009). It is in her essay for a collection on Jean-Luc Nancy (Guibal and Martin, 2004) that she addresses Sartre's works more prominently, with particular emphasis on Sartre's existential psychoanalysis, in which he analyzes quality as the revelation of being, in a section under that title. Malabou's essay, entitled, "Pierre Loves Horranges: Levinas-Sartre-Nancy: An Approach to the Fantastic in Philosophy," was subsequently translated for *Umbr(a),* a journal on psychoanalysis and culture. Malabou introduces the fantastic to account for ontological difference after Heidegger. Our focus in this paper is to interpret the significance of Sartre in Malabou's treatment of the philosophical fantastic by examining this essay. Its title, "Pierre Loves Horranges", is taken directly from a passage in *Being and Nothingness*, in the section on quality. In the passage, Sartre uses Pierre, who has numerous appearances in the text (including the most famous one about his absence), to explore how qualities make existence possible. Malabou is particularly interested in the more than symbolic ways being relates to things, and argues that it is in this relation that the real in ontological difference is revealed, what she calls the "philosophical fantastic." Calling attention to Malabou's concept of plasticity in shaping her notion of the fantastic, we trace her selective reading of the viscous in Sartre's discussion of quality, and offer a more complete analysis of existential psychoanalysis as developed in *Being and Nothingness*. In so doing we seek to underscore Sartre's concern for the ethical throughout his ontology, a concern echoed in his own account of the fantastic in his essay on Blanchot, but is largely ignored by Malabou. We also seek to show the value of re-reading Sartre in light of Malabou, to explore the question of why "Pierre loves oranges and has a horror of water", which, Sartre believes, would be the proper disclosure of psychoanalysis for the future.

Sartre's Existential Psychoanalysis

To understand why Malabou finds Sartre's existential psychoanalysis particularly useful in bringing out the fantastic in philosophy, we must first examine Sartre's position on the subject. The early Sartre's integration of psychology with ontology in *Being and Noth-*

ingness was foreshadowed by Husserl's *Phenomenological Psychology* and to a lesser extent, William James's *Philosophical Psychology*. Sartre, writing against Freudian psychoanalysis, took a new direction. He understood that the fundamental problem of human freedom – for example, his own choice to be a writer, as well as seemingly whimsical choices of matters of taste and individual desires, such as a preference for dark chocolate, roses, or black coffee – cannot be understood without a philosophical account of the most fundamental human choices. Even though Sartre insists that we exist freely and that every moment of our existence is constituted by a free choice, this does not lead him to conclude that our actions are therefore thoroughly capricious and unpredictable, rendering it impossible to comprehend human lives as a unified totality. Quite the contrary, Sartre argues that our actions, far from being mercurial or haphazard, are typically organized around immediate goals that are pursued for the sake of numerous layers of more basic goals, which ultimately reflect our most fundamental project. This project, says Sartre, represents our primordial choice of being-in-the-world. We choose our actions in such a way as to express ultimately this fundamental choice. In this way human actions conform to a unifying principle – a fundamental attitude – that allows us to explain a person's life as a whole. What is needed, says Sartre, is a method by which to conduct a "regressive analysis" of tracing particular actions to the final project that is pursued for its own sake (Sartre 1984, 589). Sartre refers to this way of understanding a person by uncovering her or his fundamental choice as "Existential Psychoanalysis."

Whereas Freudian psychoanalysis attempts to explain our actions by appealing to the unconscious, Sartre's analysis is existential in that it focuses on the way in which our actions manifest our fundamental choice of existence. Furthermore, it is a method that seeks to reveal a choice of which we have pre-reflective awareness. It is crucial to bring direct awareness to this inherent choice if we are to work toward changing it. So deeply rooted is this fundamental choice in shaping our everyday choices and defining the way we live, altering it would require nothing less than a "radical conversion" (Sartre 1984, 598).

Sartre believes that a radical conversion is needed because our fundamental project is typically a flawed project founded on bad faith. As lack of being, we desire being. Specifically, we desire to possess the full identity, density, and positivity that things exhibit, without surrendering our consciousness and freedom. Indeed, we strive to be at once a freedom-thing. We seek to escape from our own nothingness and contingency by incorporating, without compromising our consciousness and freedom, the substantiality and full positivity of the in-itself. As Sartre puts it, our most fundamental choice is the pursuit of the ideal union of in-itself-for-itself, viz. God. However, such a project is both inauthentic and unattainable, inauthentic because it betrays our existence as pure nothingness, and unattainable because the very idea of a freedom-thing is but a hopeless contradiction that can never be realized.

In spite of the impossible nature of our fundamental project, Sartre believes that we nevertheless persist in our attempt to appropriate, if only symbolically, the desirable thing-like qualities of the in-itself within our being. But even as we endeavor in this doomed project, things possess an obtrusive and inexhaustible fullness of being that is as over-whelming as it is absurd. As Sartre shows in *Nausea*, Roquentin discovers the infinite ex-cess of existence, the totality of spellbound nature. He notices the gratuitous presence of things, in their "frightful, obscene nakedness". There is always more to them than what is revealed through our momentary grasp of them. They exist in their abundance – as "mon-strous masses, all in disorder" – beyond their instrumental manifestations to consciousness (Sartre 1964, 127).

Roquentin's startling discovery would pave the way for an elaborate ontology in *Be-ing and Nothingness,* in which Sartre develops the distinctive characteristics of the for-itself and the in-itself, as well as the peculiar relation between them. As nothingness, conscious-ness is pure flux that becomes consciousness-of-something by projecting itself toward some object. The transcendent object which fills consciousness and gives it its content, is the in-itself. Consciousness thus approaches every entity in the world, even other subjects, "positionally" in a subject-to-object relation. The bond between subject and object is a delicate one. As consciousness, I experience the world by turning everything around me, including other consciousness, into a passive unity of objects. All things are defined by their instrumentality with respect to my chosen projects. But by the same token, I am quite dependent and even vulnerable to these objects in so far as consciousness demands as its very support their being-there. It is through their presence that my existence as conscious-ness-of-something is sustained. Furthermore, because consciousness, as pure nothingness, is thoroughly translucent, the for-itself is in no position to posit or found the being of the substantial object of which it is conscious. Hence, the object must exist transphenomenally, as brute being, independent of and prior to its encounter with consciousness. It must have been already-there before consciousness could nihilate it toward a project at hand, objecti-fying it in the process. As we will show, Malabou would later adopt this ontological realism to support her view on the fantastic.

Sartre further argues that, whereas we encounter the amorphous, massive being of the in-itself, things *appear* to us in limited perspectives through the lenses of our specific projects. We engage in patterns of bad faith by acting in ways that symbolically place our-selves as the foundation of the in-itself, and deceptively justify our existence as the source of the in-itself. A common mechanism is appropriation, in which I attempt to possess the object completely so that it may become a part of me. Possession is therefore symbolic of the impossible union of in-itself-for-itself, the fundamental project that informs and unifies our actions. In this way, our fundamental project "arranges the world with its meaning, its instrumental-complexes, and its coefficient of adversity" (Sartre 1984, 598). Since the possessive acts are part of our spontaneous, lived experience, we do not necessarily know or understand their connection to our basic desire "to have", which amounts to the hopeless project to be God. It is the task of existential psychoanalysis to bring about such awareness.

Sartre further points out that this fundamental desire to appropriate objects is reflected not only in our actions but more profoundly in our attitude or "gut feelings" toward things. Our attitude toward a given object – e.g., whether it invokes exhilaration or disgust – depends to a large extent on whether or not it exhibits for us any possessable quality. Sartre observes that the things we find most revolting are those that offer the strongest resistance toward us. Such are objects with a "slimy" or viscous quality. To develop this point, Sartre identifies three general states in objects: liquid, solid, and the ambiguous quality in between, slime. Liquid and solid things are ideal objects of possession. The translucency of water, for instance, gives me the kind of satisfaction that comes with the appropriation of knowledge. Like consciousness, water has the clarity to reveal something without changing its actual identity. On the other hand, solid things, such as a rock, have the unmistakable opacity that fastens them as non-evasive, accessible objects. The rock's concreteness allows me to modify it at will, making it uniquely my possession. But none of this can be said of slimy entities. To use Sartre's example of honey, when I dip my finger into a jar of honey, it clings to me and slowly glides down my finger like a snake. And when I try to squeeze it, it oozes out like worms between my fingers. All told, "Slime is the revenge of the In-itself," one that symbolizes "the sugary death of the For-itself" (Sartre 1984, 777).

Existential psychoanalysis thus allows us to explain not only the coherence and unity of our freely chosen action, but also our attitude, feelings, and preferences toward particular things we encounter. Returning to his example of Pierre, Sartre argues that it is by conducting an existential psychoanalysis on Pierre's actions and dispositions, to trace them through concentric layers of secondary and primary projects to reveal his fundamental choice of being, that we can finally understand why he is attracted to certain qualities while repulsed by others, or why he likes oranges but refuses to eat beans (Sartre 1984, 770).

Sartre and Malabou on the Fantastic

Even though Sartre believes that our desire to appropriate the in-itself underlies our entire way of being, he nevertheless maintains that, as free subjects, it is within our power to abandon our fundamental project to be God. To be sure, altering our fundamental project, and thus our entire way of being, is a drastic and difficult choice. As Sartre says, it would involve a radical conversion. In many instances, such a conversion requires not only our resolve but also our imagination. In his essay on Blanchot, originally published in *Situations* I, "Aminadab or the Fantastic Considered as a Language," Sartre offers a way of reimagining our relationship to the in-itself. Picking up the central theme of his earlier novel, *Nausea*, in which Roquentin experiences the spellbound totality of the in-itself as disorderly, "monstrous masses", Sartre reconfigures this theme in terms of the rich, over-flowing possibilities that the disorderliness of the in-itself offers up. The fantastic feeds on this disorderliness. Like the gratuitous presence of the in-itself he described in *Nausea*, Sartre states that one "cannot impose limits on the fantastic; either it does not exist at all, or else it extends throughout the universe" (Sartre 1962, 61-62). The fantastic dwells in a "topsy-turvy world" where ends are crushed and devoured by their own means, where objects reveal themselves "with an indiscipline and disorderly power" (Sartre 1962, 63). The fantastic world thus stands in stark contrast to the familiar "right-side-up world" we inhabit. Orderly and rational, things in the right-side-up world are determined by their instrumentality, their usefulness for our purposes. As Sartre puts it, this world represents the in-itself as "a piece of domesticated matter." Through our mastery over domesticated objects, we seek to escape our own contingency by symbolically appropriating them and positioning ourselves as the foundation of their being.

By contrast, the topsy-turvy world invites us to transcend the right-side-up world by engaging in its fantastic disorderliness. Things in this world are no longer purposeful objects at our disposal, subject to our whim and will. They exhibit "a kind of coarse independence that suddenly snatches their end from us just when we think we have it fast" (Sartre 1962, 65). The fantastic is unpredictable and chaotic, existing in abandonment without rhyme or reason. But here, Sartre is careful to remind us that "the fantastic is only one of a hundred ways of mirroring…(our) own image" (Sartre 1962, 64). It redirects us to our own human condition, to the reality that we exist as thoroughly contingent beings without any necessary foundation or justification for our existence. In Sartre's view, Kafka is a master of the fantastic by creating riveting, disorderly worlds to reveal powerfully our deep-seated anxiety over our own condition. He maintains that, for Kafka, "a transcendental reality certainly existed, but it was beyond our reach and served only to give us a sharper feeling of man's abandonment in the realm of the human" (Sartre 1962, 63). Interpreting Sartre's notion of the fantastic in this way allows us to see that, ultimately, what is important to him is that the fantastic holds a key to human authenticity.

This analysis shows the consistent ethical theme that underlies Sartre's works, from his depiction of existence as such in *Nausea*, to his account of existential psychoanalysis in *Being and Nothingness,* and finally to his treatment of the fantastic in *Situations*. Sartre was concerned about the tendency for us to resort to bad faith to escape the human condition when we need to be authentic. As far as he is concerned, not only are our bad faith projects doomed to failure, but more importantly, we are not in a position to promote a freer society for all until we accept our own freedom and contingency, even at utmost existential cost.

Sartre's existential psychoanalysis has certainly captured Malabou's interest, but not for the obvious reason that it is a psychoanalysis that compels us to recognize and accept the burden of human existence. Rather, Malabou attempts to draw upon the basic ontology that underlies Sartrean psychoanalysis, particularly the "there-ness" of the In-itself, to reimagine ontological difference after Heidegger. In Malabou's view, such reimagination would allow for a deeper understanding of the other, of time, suffering, technology and culture. Her book, *The Heidegger Change,* was published in France in the same year as her Sartre essay (2004), and the two works share similar subtitles that invoke the fantastic in philosophy. For the former, it is "On the Fantastic in Philosophy", and the latter, "An Approach to the Fantastic in Philosophy." The fantastic, which appears throughout Malabou's work, is never static by definition and is always associated with the *real of* ontological difference. Malabou's treatment of the fantastic represents her revision of Heideggerian change, and along with that a new ontology, one that, by her own admission, owes a debt to Sartre's genius (Malabou 2006, 109). This is true even though her account of the fantastic, as we seek to show, takes on a different focus from Sartre's. She arduously weaves Heidegger's account of change, transformation, and metamorphosis – the triad of *Wandel, Wandlung*, and *Verwandlung* – through the early and later Heidegger texts. Simply put, the fantastic is both the ontological marker and the producer of difference. Malabou summarizes ontological difference as precisely "the sameness of being, essence, and beings, *(it) is our world itself.*" (Malabou 2011a, 177).

The Heidegger Change thus embarks on a provocative and contested metaphysical quest to work out exactly how change is the real effects of existence. On Malabou's view, Heidegger's shortcoming lies in his inability to present a *visible* ontological difference. To address this problem, Malabou presents her own concept of plasticity to rehabilitate Heidegger's account of being as change. She first discussed temporal plasticity in her work on Hegel before turning to ontological plasticity in Heidegger. She refers to Heidegger's notions of *Gestell and Ereignis*, as "the gift and circulation of sameness – simultaneity and co-belonging." They are the "metabolic holding together, …(not a rigid but) a plastic phenomenal crossing of things" (Malabou 2011a, 176). But if metaphysics is to change into its other, allowing for what Malabou insists is the *real* of ontological difference, then she must explain the "double sense" that is required, namely, the objectification of ontological difference and the negation of the objectification. Malabou describes the objectification in the first sense as "being made the object of beings in the enframing," and the negation in the second sense as the "liberation of the ontological difference, as its (fantastic) coming into print on things" (Malabou 2011a, 177). Making use of her notions of plasticity and the fantastic, Malabou reconfigures Heidegger's ontology after postmodernism, to foreground its dynamic nature by calling attention to the real of ontological difference in terms of objectification and liberation. Change is therefore put in play in her re-visioning, as it were, of Heidegger: namely, as displacing itself, as visibly reasserting itself, and as becoming what it is not in order to be.

The Fantastic: Imaging the Real as Visible

Malabou would draw upon Sartre's understanding of qualities as they are revealed in being to bolster her post-Heideggerian account of change. Before examining her Sartre essay to develop this point, we must first examine two curious endnotes on Sartre that appear in *The Heidegger Change*. The first note is in the chapter entitled, "The Fantastic is Only Ever an Effect of the Real." If the fantastic is not the *real* but an effect of the *real* as the title indicates, how is the fantastic accessible to thought? As noted before, Malabou believes that fantastic thinking must think through the Heideggerian triad (*Wandel, Wandlung*, and *Verwandlung)*, and the two modalities of ontological difference (objectification and liberation). Most importantly, she also stresses that *"(i)t can only imagine what it thinks"*(Malabou 2011a, 182) . The kind of imagining required for the apprehension of ontological difference is not merely Heidegger's notion of the imagination as nihilation, but one that necessarily involves imaging the real as visible. This is where the fantastic comes in: "*The fantastic is another dimension, that of the real image of thingness*" (Malabou 2011a, 182). Turning to Sartre to support this point, she refers the readers to her essay on Sartre to explain the paradoxical phrase, "the real image of thingness". The point of her essay, she says, is to draw attention to the philosophical fantastic in Sartre by showing how Sartre allows the "real effect of existence" in such things as the roots of a chestnut tree to manifest itself. For these existents, every modification they undergo reveals the ontico-ontological difference in their new form. Notice that, in her reading of the fantastic in Sartre, Malabou has shifted the focus away from the For-itself toward the In-itself, the very things that, by already being-there, sustain the For-itself's existence as consciousness-of-something.

The second endnote appears near the conclusion of *The Heidegger Change*, in the chapter, "Man and *Dasein,* Boring Each Other". Drawing upon Heidegger's later lectures on metaphysics, Malabou analyzes the Event of Existence. As she proclaims, "Today, existence for itself, existence on recess from man is the genuine event, *Ereignis*. It is 'suddenly unveiled'" (2011a, 266). But how is it that existence, the genuine event, is revealed? To answer this question, Malabou again refers to Sartre's novel, *Nausea*, in which Roquentin confronts existence squarely without conditions. "In a sense," she states, "the only thing the novel contends with is this metamorphosis of existence into an event" (Malabou 2011a, 325). What the "crowd of metamorphoses" ultimately revealed to Roquentin is that "to exist is simply *to be there"* (Sartre 1964, 131). The revelation of the being-there of existence is indeed an event, an Ereignis. Derived from the German verb, *erreichen*, which means to put something in a state of being reached, Ereignis captures quite aptly the disclosure of the there-ness of existence.[2]

As noted above, Malabou reconstructs the fantastic in Sartre to take Heideggerian ontology in a new direction, one that would account for the real of ontological difference. For her, every change, which is also an exchange, is suffused with images (2011a, 71). What is needed is a new theory of imagination to make visible ontological transformations. "At issue," she claims, "is knowing if philosophy can, at the end of the day, endure the trial of its own experience, the becoming visible – fantastically visible – of ontological transformability; if it can accept the revelation of its destiny" (Malabou 2011a, 270). Again, it is in Sartre's early ontology and literary work that Malabou finds a useful imaginary schema for re-visioning the (ex)change, a re-vision that allows for the "fantastically visible" in beings to emerge from Being.

As so it is that her essay on Sartre, "Pierre Loves Horranges", is primarily an attempt to "situate the question of the fantastic in philosophy" (Malabou 2006, 103). The essay references *Nausea* but centers mainly on Sartrean ontology as developed in *Being and Nothingness*. In the section called "Being and Having," Sartre gives a phenomenological description of quality that captures, for Malabou, existence as the reality of ontological difference. But why does the ontological category of existence persist in philosophy long

---

[2] For Malabou, the unveiling of the *real* of ontological difference is to push ontology beyond the very line Heidegger draws between existence and its metamorphosis. Whether or not this is successful depends upon the nature of philosophy. If philosophy, in and after Heidegger, is thought turning back on itself in the journey of Being, and in this unfolding must carry within it its own challenge, it is an endeavor that is both deeply philosophical and anti-philosophical at once. For Malabou, this is the change (and the (ex)change) of ontological difference.

after Heidegger, Sartre, and Deconstruction? Malabou's answer is found, in part, by infusing Sartre's work on quality into her own notion of the fantastic.[3] She understands the fantastic as the effects of the real, the remnants of being as it undergoes change. It is not static, but the dynamic eruption of difference in existence, or, as Malabou puts it, "the real irruption of the extraordinary" (Malabou 2006, 103). On her view, the fantastic could only emerge in philosophy after Deconstruction and its predecessors, for it requires a "new signification of existence", post-*Dasein*, that addresses change, disruption, and displacement. Its task is to reveal the extraordinary emerging from the displacement of the ordinary in existence.

But what can be said of existence in the post-Heidegger era? For Malabou, this is answered, in a preliminary way, in *Nausea*. Praising Sartre's ontological realism as "the future of a certain phenomenology", she claims that existence is not limited to *Dasein* but, as Sartre describes, "enters into presence everywhere, always there, like the root of the chestnut tree, viscous paste" (Malabou 2006, 114). Malabou expands on this point by appealing to her own concept of plasticity. Plasticity allows for the changing nature of being, the slipping into and out of formlessness, the site "where metaphysics and an other thought cross and organize the modalities of their exchanges; where, for example, the trace of ontological difference forms itself, materializes itself in forms" (Malabou 2006, 114). Relating this idea to Sartre's works, Malabou notes that these forms include artistic ones, "heretofore unknown forms of philosophical writing…evidenced in texts such as *Nausea*, certain passages from *Being and Nothingness, Existence and Existents,* or *Corpus*, the first examples of a fantastic philosophy" (Malabou 2006, 114). In this fantastic philosophy, imagination becomes an artistic form to image the real. Sartre thus displaces the Heideggerian notion of imagination by unveiling the real effect of existence, viz., the real image of thingness. In this way, ontological difference "constitutes" thinking itself (Malabou 2006, 104). Malabou tells us that Sartre's first bold move toward a philosophy of the fantastic was to reinterpret *Dasein* as human reality, from which he produced a viable ontology that integrates but also overcomes Heidegger by returning to the materiality of difference. We see that move in *Nausea*, where Sartre offers a powerful imaginary schema for the becoming (fantastically) visible of ontological transformability. Sartre would provide a more developed ontological schema in *Being and Nothingness*, in connection with his account of existential psychoanalysis.

---

[3] In an important endnote she defines the fantastic in terms of the Heidegger problem and as "what returns when the category of 'existence' has disappeared from Heidegger's thought – which happens very quickly, right after *Being and Time*" (Malabou, 2011a, 116).

The Viscous as Ontological Schema

For Malabou, Sartre's ontological schema is, first and foremost, one that identifies qualities as the *objective* symbols of being, in keeping with his ontological realism. As Sartre states, the task of the psychoanalysis of things is "to establish the way in which each thing is the *objective* symbol of being and of the relation of human reality to this being" (Malabou 2006, 108). This, says Malabou, is precisely the fantastic transformative of things as symbols of the what-is-there, symbols that self-reference rather than point away from themselves. Sartre illustrates this with a discussion of viscosity. Quoting Sartre, Malabou agrees that the viscous "does not symbolize a psychic attitude *a priori*; it manifests a certain relation of being with itself and this relation has an originally psychic quality" (Malabou 2006, 109). For Sartre and Malabou, then, the viscous is given *a priori* to consciousness as a pure image that is invested with " a valid ontological schema" for all viscous existents, a schema that "will interpret the meaning of being of all the existents of a certain category," namely, all viscous things (Malabou 2006, 109).

But how does the ontological schema come into being? It does so within the very existents it schematizes. As Malabou maintains, "the viscous, as schema, is itself viscous, and it is in this sense that it shows itself as the relation of being to itself" (Malabou 2006, 109). The 'objective symbol', she notes, "designates the incoercible resistance of the real, and thus of existence, to the symbol"(Malabou 2006, 109). Paradoxically, in its resistance, the symbol both exists and is negated. Malabou uses Sartre's description of viscosity in his example of the honey-filled spoon and pot to develop this point. "The honey which slides off my spoon on to the honey contained in the jar first sculptures the surface by fastening itself on it in relief, and its fusion with the whole is presented as a gradual sinking, a collapse which appears at once as a deflation" (Malabou 2006, 109). According to Malabou, this image of the spoonful of honey sliding and sinking into the honey in the pot best captures the relation between the being of the viscous and the viscous thing. The viscous and the honey, in their formlessness yet their capacity to take on form, in their collapse and expansion as "indifferent sugared difference," represent "ontological difference at once annulled and revealed" (Malabou 2006, 109). Sartre achieved the fantastic in philosophy by making ontological difference exist, and only then, says Malabou, could there be a "metaphysical coefficient of lemon" (Malabou 2006, 110). And here she returns to the example of Pierre. Sartre contends that existential psychoanalysis holds the key to understanding, for instance, Pierre's love for oranges but repulsion toward oysters. His psychoanalysis is not merely about the apprehension of quality, or the appearance of quality in existence. It attempts to understand the relationship between beings and quality by examining how the real is revealed in quality. But most importantly, Malabou returns the discussion here to the main focus that Sartre intends for his ontology; namely, the human condition. Ultimately, she says, psychoanalysis reveals how the apprehension of quality attempts a failed escape from existence, as we seek "to pierce through the shell of nothingness about the 'there is' and to penetrate to the pure in-itself" (Malabou 2006, 110).

For Sartre and Malabou, then, psychoanalysis holds the promise of revealing the unity of being, the apprehension of quality, and the fundamental project. It is through this revelation that we can arrive at "the metaphysical coefficient" of lemon, water, oil and other entities. If psychoanalysis can show us the way the real is revealed in quality, only then can the relationship between beings and qualities be understood, only then, someday, as Sartre writes, could we hope to understand "why Pierre loves oranges and has a horror of water, why he gladly eats tomatoes and refuses to eat beans, why he vomits if he is forced to swallow oysters or raw eggs" (Sartre 1984, 770).

Conclusion

In this paper we examined the notion of the fantastic in Sartre, a topic that has mostly remained unexplored in Sartrean scholarship. We also examined Malabou's use of Sartrean ontology to develop her own view of the philosophical fantastic as the real of ontological differences, in her attempt to re-vision Heidegger's account of change. This is done by taking Sartrean psychoanalysis in a slightly different direction, focusing on the "there-ness" of the In-itself. But while Malabou acknowledges Sartre's main concern, in offering an alternative psychoanalytic theory, to address our bad faith fundamental project to be freedom-thing, she does not pursue the ethical implications of that ill-fated project. Sartre sees Pierre, and each of us, as a useless passion. It is his hope that existential psychoanalysis, whose task is to uncover the unifying principle of a person's life, will one day help us to make sense of Pierre's attitude, choices, preferences, and even his predisposition toward objects and qualities.

Sartre's own faith in the value of existential psychoanalysis can be seen in his biographies of Baudelaire, Genet, and, of course, Flaubert. In each case, he diligently applied his psychoanalytic method to explain his subject's life as a whole. If Sartre were writing today, he might be interested to probe why Malabou turned to philosophy rather than art; why she writes on Hegel, Heidegger, plasticity, and the fantastic in philosophy; why the concept of change is so important to her; why she is drawn to neuroscience, and why she chooses to connect neuroscience with Continental philosophy. Indeed, Sartre might be most interested in investigating why Malabou chose to neglect the ethical in her treatment of his psychoanalysis, and why his philosophy has not occupied a more prominent place in her work, even after she conceded the "genius" of his contribution. It is rather puzzling that "Pierre Loves Horranges" is her only piece of writing on Sartre to date. Moreover, the essay is not wholly about Sartre, but wedges him between two other French philosophers, Levinas and Nancy. Malabou strategically singles out Sartre's analysis of quality in *Being and Nothingness* to explain the fantastic in philosophy, all the while displacing, through omission, the more crucial aspects of his ontology concerning consciousness, freedom, and bad faith. Even though her theory of the fantastic has, by her own admission, benefitted from Sartrean ontology, Malabou has missed a golden opportunity to reveal a deconstruction inherent in that ontology, namely, in Sartre's view of humanity as a useless passion perpetually in pursuit of being, but never manages to attain a perfect coincidence with being.

We can also ask what Sartre could have learned from Malabou. Is her essay seminal for Sartreans like us, who have followed her on her journey to reveal the fantastic in philosophy? How has Malabou's reading of Sartre, as we have explicated in this paper, shaped our own re-reading of Sartre? Malabou has certainly made us more aware of the fantastic qualities of existence, exemplified, in part, by her return to Roquentin in *Nausea*. But more importantly, Malabou has invited Sartreans to look for a more dynamic, disruptive, and deconstructivist view of psychoanalysis, one that would really allow for the evolution and opposition of qualities in matters of taste as they emerge for situated existents. Future psychoanalysis is poised to seek richer explanations of the symbolic quality of Pierre's love of oranges and tomatoes, fear of water, hatred of green beans and repulsion towards oysters and raw eggs. It would examine how the associations of these qualities in Pierre's experience align with his fundamental project, and how oppositional moments, disruption and displacement of qualities, resistance and reassertion, might play a role in allowing, not even for a moment and eventually, Pierre's love for oranges to persist.

Prof. Dr. Constance L. Mui, Loyola University New Orleans, USA, cmui[at]loyno.edu
Prof. Dr. Julien S. Murphy, College of Arts and Sciences, University of Southern Maine,
Portland ME, USA, jmurphy[at]maine.edu

References

Badiou, Alain. *The Adventure of French Philosophy,* New York: Verso Press, 2012.

Guibal, Francs and Martin, Jean-Clet, eds. *Sens entous sens: autour des travaux de Jean-Luc Nancy,* Paris: Galilee, 2004)

Gutting, Gary. *Thinking the Impossible, French Philosophy Since 1960.* Oxford: Oxford University Press, 2013.

James, Ian. *New French Philosophy.* Cambridge: Polity Press, 2012.

Johnston, Adrian and Catherine Malabou, *Self and Emotional Life: Philosophy, Psychoanalysis and Neuroscience.* New York: Columbia University Press, 2013.

Malabou, Catherine. *The Future of Hegel: Plasticity, Temporality and Dialectic,* translated by Lisabeth During, New York: Routledge Press, 2004.

Malabou, Catherine. "Pierre Loves Horranges: Levinas-Sartre-Nancy: An Approach to the Fantastic in Philosophy," translated by Steven Miller for *Umbr(a),* No. 1, 2006: 103-117.

Malabou,Catherine. *Plasticity at the Dusk of Writing: Dialectic, Destruction, Deconstruction,* translated by Carolyn Shread, New York: Columbia University Press, 2009.

Malabou, Catherine. *The Heidegger Change: On the Fantastic in Philosophy,* translated by Peter Skafish, *New York:* State University of New York Press, 2011(a).

Malabou,Catherine. *Changing Difference,* translated by Carolyn Shread, Cambridge: Polity Press, 2011(b).

Malabou, Catherine. *Ontology of the Accident: An Essay on Destructive Plasticity,* translated by Carolyn Shread, Cambridge: Polity Press, 2012.

Mullarkey, John. *Post-Continental Philosophy ,* New York: Continuum Press, 2006.

Sartre, Jean-Paul. *Being and Nothingness,* translated by Hazel E. Barnes, New York: Washington Square Press, 1984.

Sartre, Jean-Paul. "'Aminadab' Or the Fantastic Considered as Language" in *Sartre: Literary and Philosophical Essays,* translated by Annette Michelson, New York: Collier Books, 1962.

Sartre, Jean-Paul. *Nausea,* translated by Lloyd Alexander. New York: New Directions Publishing Corporation, 1964.

LARS ANDRÉE (Uppsala)

Méditations sartriennes: Péripéties de la notion de vécu[1]

Sartrian Meditations: Vicissitudes of the Notion of Lived Experience

Abstract

One must have lived to write the story of his life and you must have some lived experience to describe the life of another - this may seem like a truism. However, this idea poses different questions, which are the subject of this article. For example, if we admit the general rule that one who writes about music has some knowledge of music, as the one who writes about science has some knowledge of scientific achievements, then we can conclude that the writer on literature should at least have some idea of literature. So it is surprising how Bourdieu in his book Les règles de l'art: Genèse et structure du champ littéraire *reversed this opinion. Bourdieu suggests that Sartre, being a writer, lack of the ability to understand Flaubert. For Bourdieu it is the writer's position which makes Sartre incapable of writing about literature. Through a critical reinterpretation of Bourdieu's theses, the author shows the difficulties of biographical writing as such, as well as the problems of (understanding) the Sartrean notion of lived experience and its (possible) applications.*

Keywords: Jean-Paul Sartre, Gustave Flaubert, lived experience, literature, biographical writing,

"Pour écrire l'histoire de sa vie, il faut d'abord avoir vécu; aussi n'est-ce pas la mienne que j'écris" (Musset 1989/2, 312), dit Alfred de Musset dans *La Confession d'un Enfant du Siècle*. Il peut sembler étonnant d'introduire une conférence sur Sartre à la Sorbonne avec des mots de Musset, un écrivain que je n'ai trouvé mentionné que très rarement dans les écrits de Sartre, un écrivain que Flaubert n'aimait guère et que les frères Goncourt condamnaient (Goncourt 1989, 425).

---

[1] Cet article a été présenté par le philosophe et critique d'art suédois Lars Andrée (1950-2003) d'abord comme communication à l'Ecole Internationale de Philosophie à Varna en 1992, à la suite d'une invitation de ma part. La traduction bulgare de l'article a été publiée dans la revue *Filosofski alternativi* (No. 4, 1995: 14-21). Ici nous publions la version française originale de l'article, telle que je l'ai reçue en 1993, c.-à-d. sans altération, exception faite des références qui ont été mis en accord avec les exigences de la revue *Labyrinth*. Ce texte a été présenté de même au Colloque ouvert du Groupe d'études sartriennes à l'Université de Paris – I, Sorbonne, le vendredi 25 juin 1993 [note de réd. – Yvanka B. Raynova].

Qu'il faille avoir vécu pour écrire l'histoire de sa vie ou qu'il faille avoir une certaine expérience de la vie pour décrire la vie d'une autre, que l'auteur aussi bien que son objet soient des enfants d'un temps déterminé et vivent dans un siècle précis, dans un contexte social défini – cela peut sembler être un truisme. Cependant, ces petites lignes de Musset posent la plupart des questions que j'aimerais traiter.

Si nous admettons comme règle générale que celui qui écrit sur la musique connaisse la musique, que celui qui écrit sur les sciences ait quelques connaissances des conquêtes scientifiques, alors nous pouvons conclure que celui qui écrit sur la littérature doit au moins avoir eu l'idée de faire de la littérature lui-même.

Pour les mêmes raisons, un écrivain avec un engagement actif arrive plus facilement à décrire des fonctions politiques, comme l'a fait p. ex. le poète et l'homme politique Mao Tsé-toung dans son discours de Yenan. De fait, une critique littéraire formulée par des auteurs engagés va souvent plus loin et devient plus claire qu'une critique plus académique. Dans le débat sur le réalisme, c'est Brecht qui a raison, pas Lukács.

Par conséquent, j'ai été surpris de la façon dont Bourdieu, dans *Les règles de l'art: Genèse et structure du champ littéraire* a tourné à la légère toute cette opinion. Bourdieu estime que Sartre, étant écrivain, manque de capacité de comprendre Flaubert. Pour Bourdieu c'est la position d'écrivain qui rend Sartre incapable d'écrire sur la littérature. Bourdieu considère les points de vue de Sartre simplement comme des marques de posture immanentes au champ (Bourdieu 1992, 267).

Dans l'œuvre de Bourdieu nous trouvons dans l'index des noms onze références à Jean-Paul Sartre, pour de simples mentions aussi bien que pour des paragraphes entiers. Mais, dans l'index des concepts il n'y a aucune référence au vécu ou à des notions proches.

Il y a des raisons pour s'arrêter un peu sur ce manque et sur ce qu'il signifie. En cherchant nous-mêmes le concept du vécu nous trouvons p. ex. un Baudelaire qui "a vécu, avec la lucidité des commencements, toutes les contradictions, éprouvées comme autant de *double binds*, qui sont inhérents au champ littéraire en voie de constitution... ", (ibid., 1992, 97) ou un Gautier, qui a vécu "la condition d'un 'ouvrier littéraire'" (ibid., 124).

Bref, le vécu est chez Bourdieu associé au champ, voire au marché, comme si la genèse de différents écrivains ne peut être trouvée que dans un contexte interne au champ littéraire. Mais Bourdieu estime aussi que Je vécu est presque inaccessible pour des recherches puisque nous ne pouvons pas revivre le vécu.[2]

---

[2] "Bref, on ne peut pas revivre ou faire revivre le vécu des autres, et ce n'est pas la sympathie qui conduit à la compréhension véritable, c'est la compréhension véritable qui conduit à la sympathie. ou, mieux, à cette sorte d'amour intellectualiste qui, fondé sur le renoncement au narcissisme, accompagne la découverte de la nécessité" (Bourdieu 1992, 417-418)

Permettez-moi de revenir quelques années en arrière. Vous connaissez certainement l'idée fondamentale de la thèse de Lukács sur le triomphe du réalisme, l'idée selon laquelle Balzac a fait une littérature réaliste malgré lui, l'idée selon laquelle la vision du monde des romans de Balzac ne correspondrait pas aux intentions de l'auteur.

Un écrivain suédois, Jan Myrdal, a examiné le fond réel de cette thèse, en comparaison avec l'œuvre de Balzac. Il a découvert que Lukács utilise, dans ses arguments, des sources incomplètes ou insuffisantes. Myrdal montre comment cette pensée directive, c'est-à-dire selon laquelle Balzac serait un grand écrivain par erreur, est proclamée par Victor Hugo, poursuivie par Jules Vallès et Friedrich Engels pour devenir finalement chez Lukács une théorie sur le triomphe du réalisme. Pour Myrdal, écrivain, cette question est primordiale et il dit:

> Ces problèmes ne concernent pas seulement les questions fondamentales pour tout écrivain: le souci d'être conscient de son travail, la forme – le contenu, et de vouloir, à tort ou à raison, défendre son intégrité; ils concernent aussi notre aptitude à saisir quel est l'âge exact de notre époque (Mydral 1981, 98).

Nous avons fait une présentation de Myrdal et de son étude sur Balzac, qui va être publiée dans la revue *Europe*. Il est évident que nous pouvons repousser Lukács en retournant aux sources. Or, il devrait aussi être possible, comme une sorte d'entretien intellectuel, de repousser son idée à l'aide d'arguments philosophiques, car la pensée de Lukács n'est qu'une formulation d'un problème qui est beaucoup plus crucial.

Le temps présent est fascinant. Comme nous le savons, tout l'"establishement" intellectuel et toute la critique littéraire dans les pays de l'Europe de l'Est sont en mouvement. Les intellectuels rament de toutes leurs forces pour avoir de nouveau le vent dans les voiles. À l'école philosophique de Varna en 1992, le bulgare Alexander Atanassov fait explicitement allusion à Lukács quand, dans son discours intitulé *Entre la cage et la jungle* (Atanassov 1992, 184-190), il essaie de sauver la littérature plus ou moins communiste pour le temps à venir. Nous pouvons y voir la métamorphose d'une façon de penser. Pour Atanassov, Lukács existe avant et après et sa thèse lui donne le pont à traverser.

Chez Ismaïl Kadaré, aussi bien connu que renommé, nous pouvons voir le résultat achevé, une sorte de simplicité pure, quand il écrit:

> La dictature et la littérature véritable ne peuvent cohabiter que d'une façon: en se dévorant nuit et jour l'une l'autre. L'écrivain est l'ennemi naturel de la dictature (Kadaré 1991, 9).

Je n'estime pas du tout que Pierre Bourdieu soit ainsi naïf mais il exprime le même esprit d'une manière un peu plus subtile ou illusoire, quand il dit à la fois que l'on ne peut pas "reconstruire une vision du monde" à partir d'une œuvre littéraire, que cette tâche est "insolite, voire impossible" (Bourdieu 1992, 437) et que l'analyse sociale que présente Flaubert dans *L' Education Sentimentale* serait d'un côté "une objectivation extraordinairement réussie (et quasi scientifique) des expériences sociales" (ibid., 152), ou de l'autre "sociologique si elle n'était pas séparée d'une analyse scientifique par la forme dans laquelle elle se livre et se masque à la fois" (ibid., 59). Toute la partie où Bourdieu traite du pouvoir de l'écriture (ibid., 50ff) montre qu'il donne à l'écriture une fonction libératrice qui peut dégager des liens sociaux, des conditions sociales presque indépendamment de la prise de position de l'auteur.Cette génuflexion devant une technique narrative est chez Bourdieu prolongée par un épilogue curieux : *Pour un corporatisme de l'universel,* où il s'approche de la vue de Julien Benda sur le rôle des intellectuels dans la société, des intellectuels qui auraient collectivement une sorte d'"intérêt propre" à défendre au dessus de la mêlée (ibid., 472).

Je n'ai rien contre Bourdieu. Je trouve extrêmement agréable à lire. Chez lui chacun reconnaît son propre entourage mais l'on ne peut échapper à une sensation affligeante de déjà v u ou de déjà lu. Pourtant, l'on a envie d'engager une polémique avec lui p ex quand il déclare que "seule une analyse de la genèse du champ littéraire (…) peut conduire à une compréhension véritable" de Flaubert (ibid., 75) ou que l'intérêt que portait le père de Gustave à Montaigne le rapprocherait littérairement de son fils (ibid., 128). Ce père s'endormait lorsque son fils tenta de lui lire sa première version de *l'Éducation sentimentale* (Sartre 1988, 688). Les instruments de mesure de Bourdieu ne sont pas assez précis pour saisir le vécu et l'idéologie chez Flaubert.

Avec ces outils, Bourdieu pourrait expliquer pourquoi la Sorbonne se trouve où elle se trouve, pourquoi cette galerie s'appelle Galerie Dumas et peut-être pourrait-il cerner l'origine de cette conférence et ce qu'il y a derrière l'un ou l'autre exposés que nous écoutons ici ; mais une très grande partie de la littérature et de la philosophie se trouvent hors du champ de Bourdieu. Pas une seule de ses notions ne peut par exemple expliquer ma carrière, jusqu'à la phrase que j'exprime maintenant.

Il est bien connu que, pour l'édition de *L 'Idiot de la Famille* Sartre dit qu'il a remplacé son ancienne notion de conscience par ce qu'il appelle le vécu.[3] Dans une thèse, l'allemande Monika Schulten (Schulten 1988) soulevé plusieurs indications qui montrent cette

---

[3] Sartre écrit p.ex. dans les *Situations IX*: "...j'ai remplacé mon ancienne notion de conscience - bien que j'utilise encore beaucoup le mot - par ce que j'appelle le vécu" (Sartre 1972, 108).

transfiguration du monde des notions de Sartre. Peut-être pourrait-on ici parler d'un véritable tournant de la pensée de Sartre. Cependant, je ne le crois pas.

Déjà dans *Les Carnets de la Drôle de Guerre* Sartre esquisse de façon clairvoyante comment l'interprétation de Rousseau pose un problème pour lui (Sartre 1983, 358). En résumé, Sartre y écrit que l'on peut, premièrement, établir un lien de compréhension entre l'origine genevoise de Rousseau et *le Contrat social* ou, deuxièmement que l'on peut partir de la personnalité de Rousseau pour montrer que s'il écrivait un *Contrat social,* il devrait l'écrire tel ou, troisièmement que l'on peut ramener l'ouvrage à des idées antérieures de Rousseau.

Si nous expliquons Rousseau par Genève, la-personnalité de Rousseau s'efface comme Haubert s'efface dans la description de Bourdieu.

Si nous isolons un modèle des autres, *le Contrat* devient strictement individuel et incomparable, une pure affaire de psychologie ou de logique.

Le problème qui consiste pour Sartre à multiplier et à unifier ces points de vue opposés se présente déjà ici, mais ce ne sera que dans les études de Flaubert qu'il avance vers une solution. Dans l'analyse du vécu il unit les différents aspects.

Dans la diversité troublante de *L'idiot de la Famille,* nous allons trouver que pratiquement chaque partie possède un, et seulement un noyau, et que celui-ci est toujours exprimé en termes de vécu.

Nous n'avons qu'à suivre l'utilisation et le développement de cette notion dans l'œuvre pour commencer à saisir une idée de la portée diversifiée, ambiguë et fertile de cette notion. Voici quelques repères:

A. Les affections de Gustave "sont *vécues* pleinement et vaguement sans que personne soit là pour les vivre..." (Sartre 1971a, 2)·

B. Gustave "...tient son enfance pour la vérité profonde de ses quinze ans. C'est elle, inoubliable, inoubliée, qui l'a fait ce qu'il est devenu : elle reste en lui toujours actuelle, mais ce n'est pas tant la réalité *vécue* de son présent qu'un axe universel de référence ..." (ibid., 30).

C. "Cette double appartenance simultanée de l'âme au monde, du monde à l'âme, Flaubert l'appelle, quand elle fait l'objet d'une expérience concrète et *vécue,* tout simplement la Poésie" (ibid., 33). " ...La poésie est une aventure silencieuse de l'âme, un événement *vécu* qui est sans commune mesure avec le langage..." (ibid., 35).

D. "Que la réalité soit syncrétisme ou synthèse, existence au jour le jour *vécue* ou brusque reprise de soi-même et du monde dans une appropriation mystique, elle se place en deçà ou au-delà de l'analyse verbale ..." (ibid., 37).

E. " ...parler est, chez tous, une expérience immédiate et spontanée, *vécue,* dans la mesure où la parole est une conduite; inversement le *vécu* n'est jamais vierge de mots ... " (ibid., 38).

F. "Et puis, si l'occasion l'exige, il faudra reconnaître que l'amour *vécu* ne peut se nommer sans se réinventer. On changera l'un par l'autre le discours et le *vécu* " (ibid.).

G. "...les écrits de Flaubert adolescent corroborent entièrement les souvenirs de sa mère ; ils nous permettent d'entrevoir l'expérience primitive telle qu'elle a été *vécue* du dedans.../ ---/ Gustave, avec un sens profond de ses v rais problèmes - ce qu'il ne faut pas confondre avec la lucidité - met aussitôt le doigt sur l'événement fondamental de sa proto-histoire ... " (ibid., 40).

H. "...le flot du *vécu* ne cesse de rouler des mots, pêle-mêle, tantôt les maintenant à la surface et tantôt les engloutissant pour les charrier invisibles entre deux eaux" (ibid., 41).

C'est excitant de rassembler ainsi un bouquet de citations de la notion du vécu dans *L'idiot de la Famille.* Je vous ai fait un bouquet de sept jolies fleurs et je ne suis qu'à la page 41, et nous savons que chaque utilisation du vécu chez Sartre condense un épisode, une évolution ou une pensée de Flaubert. Les citations ci-dessus résument l'épisode où l'on dit à Gustave:

"Va voir... à la cuisine si j'y suis", et nous aboutirons au rapport initial de Gustave avec les mots. Nous pourrions croire que le vécu, pour Sartre, est un trou noir, un gouffre énorme constamment ouvert dans le coin droit du tympan de Sartre sur l'idiot de la famille, Gustave Flaubert.

Comment devons-nous interpréter et comprendre le vécu chez Sartre? À travers l'intérieur de Sartre? Par une autopsie phénoménologique? Dans une œuvre romanesque?

Ou à travers l'extérieur? À travers Flaubert? Par un procédé purement académique? Le sujet est gigantesque. Je ne peux qu'indiquer quelques-unes des pistes que je suis dans mon travail.

Un problème est évidemment que le vécu est extrêmement mobile, fragile et que "le flot du vécu" (ibid., 646) ne cesse jamais. Tant qu'il y a un vécu il est rempli petit à petit de nouvelles impressions, de nouvelles perceptions, de nouveaux éléments qui ont tout de suite une coloration affective et qui s'intègrent dans une union synthétique d'un vécu dans une constante totalisation.

Tout ce processus se fait spontanément et au moins dans la première analyse sans que le vécu ait quelque véritable influence sur le processus. Les impressions affirment parfois le vécu, ou bien, généralement, l'existence du vécu est en permanence sous pression, sous domination extérieure, sous menace.

Notons que Sartre ne donne priorité à aucun "niveau" spécifique du vécu, ni même le vécu du vécu. Des expériences privées et personnelles se mélangent sans cesse avec des impressions politiques ou avec des perceptions encore plus structurellement conditionnés.

Le vécu n'est pas la même chose que l'expérience malgré l'utilisation souvent synonyme dans les textes de Sartre. L'expérience est plutôt structurée au préalable, déjà achevée tandis que le vécu a une existence propre. Un avantage avec la notion du vécu, c'est que le mot a une autre signification que la conscience et nous échappons alors au subconscient notoirement difficile. Mais en même temps, le vécu est rempli de mémoire, c'est-à-dire d'images (Sartre 1972a, 653) et même de trous de mémoire.

En lisant *L'idiot de la Famille* attentivement, nous découvrons que le sens du vécu change en glissant ou se coagule de la première partie sur *La Constitution* avec un vécu toujours ouvert, à la partie suivante sur *La Personnalisation* avec un vécu beaucoup plus clos.

L'avenir pénètre le vécu et à propos de la scolarité de Flaubert nous pouvons lire: "Que fait-il sinon rev ivre, une à une, des minutes déjà vécues ... " (Sartre 1971b, 1137). Dans la description de Sartre, Gustave Flaubert devient à l'ouverture de la dimension du futur de plus en plus déterminé par sa protohistoire : "Le fleuve du vécu est *orienté,* il /Gustave/ le sent" (ibid., 1743).

Désormais, la chute à Pont-l'Evêque sera, en ce qui concerne le vécu, caractérisée d'un côté par le libre écoulement des sensations quand Gustave " ...tombe au niveau du pur vécu" (ibid., 1805); ce sera un monde vécu immédiatement sans structure. Or, de l'autre côté, les sensations sont déterminées : "En d'autres termes, la situation, en tant qu'elle est vécue, est déjà structurée par la totalité du passé" (ibid., 1822).

Celui qui veut appliquer Sartre à Sartre ou comprendre Sartre à travers Sartre doit implicitement ou explicitement prendre comme un des points de départ sa notion du vécu. Je pense que cela est valable pour l'ontologie, l'éthique et l'esthétique aussi bien que pour des v ues générales biographiques et des études spécialisées.

En pénétrant dans l'œuvre de Sartre, à partir de *L'idiot de la Famille,* avec le vécu dans les bagages, nous allons trouver que la notion du vécu devient sans cesse de plus en plus vaste.

Nous voyons par exemple que chaque métamorphose ou conversion dans *Saint Genet* est située au niveau du vécu.

Si nous séparons le vécu dans *L'ldiot de la Famille* de la méthode progressive-régressive nous aurons un vécu qui est proche de l'être-pour-soi. Ainsi, toutes les qualités caractéristiques que Sartre attribue à l'être- pour-soi (ou le cogito de Descartes) peuvent être transférées au vécu mais le vécu a un sens plus large. Ontologiquement le vécu occupera la même place que l'être-pour-soi et par ce fait la question, philosophiquement obscure, du rapport entre des vécus différents, la possibilité de connaître les autres, est déjà résolue.

Encore un pas en arrière. Dans *La Nausée* Sartre compose une analyse phénoménologique et romanesque du vécu et il dit que "La différence essentielle entre Antoine Roquentin et moi, c'est que moi j'écris l'histoire d'Antoine Roquentin" (Sartre 1983, 410).

En faisant une extrapolation uniquement esthétique de *L'Idiot de la Famille,* nous pouvons trouver d'abord *La Nausée* et aussi son prolongement fictif, dans un roman qui diminue d'une manière cohérente la distance entre ce qui a été vécu et la représentation du vécu. Le prochain pas dans cette course est la vie, vécue sans remaniement en une esthétique romanesque.

Pareillement, on peut dire que le vécu comprend l'analyse de l'image et puis de l'imaginaire, c'est-à-dire les rêves, la littérature etc, en même temps que cette notion du vécu dépasse synthétiquement l'image, qui est en elle-même une synthèse.

L'analyse dans *L'Idiot de la Famille* n'est naturellement pas identique à l'analyse dans *L'imaginaire* mais il est frappant de voir la fidélité de Sartre envers ses points de v us antérieurs. La distinction entre la perception et l'image est presque identique dans *L'imaginaire, Saint Genet* et *L'Idiot de la Famille.*

Dans *L'imaginaire* de 1936, Sartre écrit que "...l'objet en image n'est jamais rien de plus que la conscience qu'on en a" (1986, 37), et que les images sont des fictions (ibid., 46). Un des clous de *L'idiot de la Famille* est de montrer qu'il n'y a rien dans *Madame Bovary* qui n'était pas déjà dans le vécu de Gustave Flaubert. Les points, les virgules, les personnages et la politique, tout peut du moins en théorie, être déduit de Flaubert.

L'œuvre implique toujours l'auteur, mais l'implication opposée n'est pas valable car alors l'auteur ne serait pas libre de créer son œuvre. L'écrivain possède la liberté que l'œuvre n'a jamais. Dans *L'idiot de la Famille* Sartre nous montre cette liberté paradoxale de Flaubert.

Cette liberté peut être exprimée par les mots: "Pour ouvrir ma porte, j'ai tout un jeu de clés" (Doubrovsky 1989, 69), que Serge Doubrovsky écrit dans *Le Livre brisé.* Une centaine de pages après, nous lisons dans un passage central de ce roman inventif, qu'on peut s'écrire une enfance d'après une multitude de recettes dont les plus accessibles pour un écrivain aujourd'hui sont p ex de "transformer moi-même en moi-mythe, à la Rousseau ", ou de "faire un apologue moral, à la Gide" ou le "cuisiner à la Freud", ou "épicier à la Marx". En un mot: "Dans une enfance, il y en a pour tous les goûts." (ibid., 269).

J'ai travaillé comme professeur de philosophie, de littérature comparée et de la langue suédoise dans des lycées suédois pendant plusieurs années. Parmi mes élèves, il y avait une fille qui s'appelle Eva. En classe elle a lu *Madame Bovary* et puis elle a commencé à collectionner des phrases qui lui plaisaient d'une manière intime. Elle a trouvé la phrase suivante écrite sur un radiateur, dans un train: "L'intermédiaire n'admet pas la température moyenne." En voyant cela j'ai compris qu'elle était en train de transformer sa scolarité en un amphigouri.

Nous avons ensuite étudié *La Nausée* et pour cette raison ses problèmes ont changé. Un jour elle m'a dit: "Je me pose la question suivante: que se passera-t-il si je meurs demain, que restera-t-il alors de moi? Quelques souvenirs isolés et rien d'autre. Voilà pourquoi je tiens un journal. Or, voilà que le problème suivant se pose: Que dois-je écrire? Qu'est-ce qui est important? Ce que je mange? Est-ce le travail pour préparer les épreuves? Ou autre chose? L'amour?"

Ce qui l'a fascinée en *Madame Bovary,* c'est que tout y est si ordinaire, si simple et en même temps si chargé de signification.

Après, elle a été très surprise quand nous avons fait une interprétation freudienne de *la Nausée* à partir de la prédilection de Roquentin, qui était de cueillir des bouts de papier et à partir de sa rencontre avec le cahier d'orthographe.

Eva n'avait pas de clés mais elle n'était pas exceptionnelle ; au contraire, elle était comme la moyenne des élèves.

La seule chose peu commune chez Eva était sa façon d'entrer par la lecture dans une névrose littéraire. Si elle avait continué, elle aurait commencé à collectionner les idées reçues ou les pseudo-pensées et elle aurait dans ce cas établi une pseudo-conscience à la Flaubert. L'anée suivante elle était prête à commencer son journal avec les mots de Sartre: "Le mieux serait d'écrire les événements au jour le jour" (Sartre 1981, 5).

Pour moi, cet exemple montre surtout que nous pouvons effectivement entrer dans le vécu des autres. Ce qu'a fait Eva d'une manière spontanée nous pouvons le faire consciemment. Comme Husserl l'a dit, le vécu de l'autre "est constitué à titre d'"alter-ego"" (Husserl 1986, 78).

La partie suivante de ma méditation, la partie finale, comme l'ensemble, je l'ai effectuée, dans l'attitude de la réduction transcendantale, c'est-à-dire où le sujet et ce qu'il traite se peignent tout entiers, sans répétition.

Eh bien, quand j'étais en train de préparer la présente intervention, mon travail a été interrompu par la mort de mon père. Le lundi 5 avril dernier, Ragnar est mort et le samedi 17 il a été enterré dans sa tombe au cimetière de Boden dans le nord de la Suède. J'étais là, avec Marianne et Erik. Bo, Karin, Kristina et Gunilla étaient là aussi. Nous étions debout dans une boue de neige, regardant en silence le cercueil s'enfoncer dans la tombe, écoutant les mots du pasteur. Nous laissions tomber, chacun à notre tour, nos bouquets de fleurs et Marianne a lu un court poème. En traversant le cimetière à nouveau, pour rentrer, le petit cortège s'est dispersé et quelques minutes plus tard, les voitures partaient dans des directions différentes. Une Mercedes 2200, d'un modèle récent, couleur crème, une Volvo Amazon 544, de l'année 1966, grise de graphite, et le corbillard, argentée.

Ensuite, Marianne, Erik et moi sommes retournés à la tombe et j'ai raconté que Ragnar avait acheté cette tombe en avril 1937 et que lui-même s'était trouvé à la tombe ouverte en septembre cette année-là pour voir sa première femme y être inhumée.

Sur la pierre tombale elle est appelée Stina. Elle est morte très jeune.

Depuis, la tombe a été ouverte à deux reprises, en 1959 et en 1962, et à chaque fois Ragnar était là, regardant sa propre tombe ouverte, voyant le gel marbrer le gravier argileux en couches claires et en couches sombres. Des cristaux de glace dans la terre suédoise.

J'avais le même âge qu'Erik aujourd'hui quand je me trouvais en 1962 à côté de Ragnar, regardant le cercueil de Maria Andrée s'enfoncer dans la terre et je savais que Nils Petter Andrée se trouvait déjà dans la tombe.

Tout est comme d'habitude: les amas de neige grisâtres dans la rue du Cimetière, les bouleaux près de la rivière gelée, la pierre tombale en marbre blanc, le trou noir, et le cercueil clair, de chêne soigneusement poli.

Une triple perspective effrayante m'a frappée: Erik se trouvait au même endroit que moi-même il y a 31 ans; moi je me trouvais au même endroit que Ragnar à cette même occasion, mais Ragnar se trouvait maintenant dans le cercueil ; Une incarnation de moi-même-trinitaire qui a duré un rien de temps, ce qui a été suffisant. C'est peut-être pour cela que l'on retourne au tombeau ; pour prêter de nos vécus aux fantômes.

Pourquoi fuirais-je?

Dr. Lars Andrée † (Uppsala University, Uppsala, Sweden)

Références

Atanassov, Alexander. "Entre la cage et la jungle", in *Philosophy and Power. Proceedings of the International Summer Philosophical Scbool*. Varna: Ministry of Education and Science, 1992, 184-190.

Bourdieu, Pierre. *Les Règles de l'art. Genèse et structure du champ littéraire*. Paris: Seuil 1992.

Doubrovsky, Serge. Le Livre brisé, Paris: Grasset, 1989.

Goncourt, Edmond et Jules de. Journal Mémoires de la Vie Littéraire II 1866-1886, Robert Laffont 1989.

Husserl, Edmond. *Méditation s cartésiennes. Introduction à la phénoménologie*, Paris: Vrin 1986.

Kadaré, Ismail. *Printemps Albanais. Chronique, lettres, réflexions*. Paris: Fayard, 1991.

Musset, Alfred de. *La Confession d'un Enfant du Siècle (avril 1834-février 1836). Œuvres complètes, tome deux*, Paris: Seuil 1989.

Myrdal, Jan. *Strindberg och Balzac. Essayer kring realismens problem* [*Strindberg et Balzac. Essais sur le problème du réalisme*], Stockholm: Norstedts, 1981.

Sartre, Jean-Paul. *Les Carnets de la Drôle de Guerre*, Paris: Gallimard 1983.

Sartre, Jean-Paul. *L'idiot de la Famille I*, Paris: Gallimard 1971a.

Sartre, Jean-Paul. *L'idiot de la Famille II*, Paris: Gallimard 1971b.

Sartre, Jean-Paul. *L'idiot de la Famille III* , Paris: Gallimard 1972a.

Sartre, Jean-Paul. *Situations IX, Sur moi-même*, Paris: Gallimard, 1972b.

Sartre, Jean-Paul. *La Nausée*, in: idem, *Œuvres romanesques*, La Pléiade, Paris: Gallimard, 1981.

Sartre, Jean-Paul. *L'imaginaire*, Gallimard (1940) 1986.

Schulten, Monika. *Jean-Paul Sartres "L'idiot de la Famille", ein methodisches Paradigma der Dichterbiographie*. Göttingen, 1988.

IN MEMORIAM

YVANKA B. RAYNOVA (Sofia/Wien)
In Memoriam Ana-Teresa Tymieniecka (1923-2014)

1. "Autonom und frei": Das Lebenscredo einer starken Persönlichkeit

In Zeiten des Internets, in denen Briefe kaum mehr per Post versandt werden und wir die Nachrichten aus anderen Kontinenten nicht erst nach Wochen erhalten, erreichen uns auch die traurigen Mitteilungen, die wir sonst vielleicht versäumt hätten, sehr schnell. So schnell, dass Einem fast unheimlich wird. So hat mich auch die Nachricht über den Tod von Ana-Teresa getroffen – schnell und unerwartet wie ein Blitzschlag.

Es scheint mir als sei es erst gestern gewesen als ich ihr zum ersten Mal begegnet bin, dabei sind es fast 30 Jahre her. Es war 1988 in Brighton, am XVIII Weltkongress für Philosophie. Für uns aus dem "Osten" war es eine Zeit des "Aufbruchs", der neuen Hoffnungen auf Veränderung durch die Perestroika. So nahm ich die Gelegenheit wahr möglichst viele Kontakte mit "westlichen" Philosophinnen und Philosophen zu knüpfen – was man heutzutage "Netzwerken" nennt und unvergleichlich leichter geworden ist – und rannte zu allen Sitzungen und Sektionen, die etwas mit Phänomenologie zu tun hatten. Es war also unabwendbar, dass ich Ana-Teresa Tymieniecka begegnete, doch es ist ihr zu verdanken, dass wir uns allmählich befreundeten. Eine günstige Voraussetzung dafür war, dass sie, im Gegensatz zu den meisten amerikanischen Philosophinnen und Philosophen, perfekt sieben Sprachen beherrschte. An den Sitzungen des World Institute for Phenomenology (WIP) war Englisch zwar die Hauptsprache und explizit erwünscht, aber man durfte auch auf Deutsch und Französisch vortragen und diskutieren. Dazu kam, dass sie durch ihre polnische Herkunft und ihre eigene Erfahrung als Emigrantin ein besonderes Verständnis für die Lage der Akademikerinnen und Akademiker aus dem "Osten" zeigte und sie auch, je nach Möglichkeit, unterstützte. In den 90er Jahren war ich z.B. mehrmals Vortragende und Mitglied des Organisationskomitees diverser Konferenzen und Kongresse des WIP. Auf ihre Einladung hin habe ich Ende 1995 einen Monat in ihrem Haus bei Boston und ihrem Landhaus in Pomfret, Vermont, verbracht, wo wir, unter anderem, das hier veröffentlichte Interview aufgenommen haben. Kurz danach hat sie mich eingeladen einen Sartre-Artikel für ihre Enzyklopädie zu schreiben (siehe Raynova 2002, 323-335). Ich habe umgehend versucht ihr abzusagen, indem ich ihr mitteilte, dass ich den Artikel nur in französischer Sprache abliefern könne und es wäre besser wenn sie mit dieser Aufgabe einen amerikanischen Sartre-Spezialisten beauftragen würde. Wenn sie sich aber etwas in den Kopf gesetzt hatte, dann konnte sie auch niemand davon abbringen. "Schick mir den Artikel auf Französisch, ich werde ihn übersetzen lassen", erwiderte sie mir.

Abgesehen davon, dass wir beide aus "Osteuropa" kamen und diverse Sprachen beherrschten, hatten wir auch etwas anderes gemeinsam – sie hatte, so wie ich, mehrere Jahre in der Schweiz und in Frankreich verbracht. Jedoch war sie begnadeter, denn sie hatte das Glück nach ihrem Studium bei Roman Ingarden zu studieren und bei Józef Bocheński in Freiburg zu dissertieren. Deshalb war eine meiner ersten Fragen, die ich ihr im persönlichen Gespräch stellte, wieso sie denn nicht in der Schweiz geblieben sei, sondern nach Amerika ausgewanderte. Sie erklärte mir, dass sie sowohl in der Schweiz, als dann auch in Paris, wo sie ihr zweites Doktorat an der Sorbonne erwarb, und auch in Belgien, wo sie einige Jahre am Europakolleg unterrichtete, als Wissenschafterin nicht wirklich ernst genommen wurde, da sie eine Frau war. Wenn man bedenkt, dass Frauen bis Ende der 70er Jahre in der Schweiz nicht einmal wählen durften, dass es in Westeuropa kaum Universitätsprofessorinnen gab, dann ist das einleuchtend. Dennoch scheint sie schon damals einen tiefen Eindruck auf ihre Professoren und Kollegen gemacht zu haben. Denn unlängst, als ich in einem Gespräch mit Kardinal Schönborn Tymieniecka erwähnte, sagte er: "Ich war damals ein junger Professor und sie auch, aber sie stand in der Hierarchie wesentlich höher. Bocheński hatte eine sehr hohe Meinung von ihr. Und wenn er etwas Gutes über jemanden sagte, dann hieß das schon viel." Die große Wertschätzung Bocheńskis konnte jedoch nicht verhindern, dass sie "Europa in Tränen verließ", wie sie mir im persönlichen Gespräch mitteilte. Sie machte sich also auf den Weg nach Amerika, wo sie glaubte, dass gegenüber Ausländern und Frauen weniger Vorurteile herrschen würden. Was mich in ihrer Erzählung so beeindruckte, war ihr Mut und ihr tiefer Glaube an sich selbst und an ihrer Mission. Am anderen Kontinent angekommen, nahm sie zuerst eine Stelle an der Universität Waterloo in Kanada an, kurz danach wurde sie Assistenzprofessorin an diversen Hochschulen und Universitäten in den USA und 1972 Professorin an der St. John University in New York. 1968 begann sie mit der Herausgabe der *Analecta Husserliana* und ein Jahr später, 1969, veranstaltete sie den ersten Phänomenologie-Kongress. In meinem 1993 aufgenommenen Interview mit ihr schildert sie diesen Weg bis hin zur Entstehung des WIP folgendermaßen:

An diesem Kongress nahm sogar Van Breda teil. Überhaupt alle älteren Phänomenologen waren anwesend. Ingarden sollte auch kommen, aber er bekam kein Visum. Im
Rahmen des Kongresses gründete ich die erste Internationale Gesellschaft für Phänomenologie. So begann unsere Arbeit. Später gründeten wir eine andere, genauso ein-
zigartige Internationale Gesellschaft für Phänomenologie und Literatur. Das war zugleich der Anfang unserer interdisziplinären Tätigkeit. 1975, am Kongress in Retz,
Italien, haben wir dann die Internationale Gesellschaft für Phänomenologie und Hu-
manwissenschaften gegründet. Somit waren alle Sektoren der Phänomenologie ge-
deckt, mit Ausnahme der biologischen Wissenschaften und der Ökologie, mit denen
wir uns heute beschäftigen. *Logos and Life* gibt diese biophysische Grundlage, natürlich auf einer philosophischen und nicht wissenschaftlichen Weise. Vor 16 Jahren habe ich das World Phenomenology Institute als eine Akademie nach dem Gesetz der
Universitäten gegründet. Somit sind wir autonom und frei (Raynova/Tymieniecka
1995, 102).

Ich glaube "autonom und frei" ist gerade das, was am besten die Persönlichkeit und
den Charakter von Ana-Teresa, so wie ich sie erlebt habe, charakterisieren würde. Sie ließ
sich schwer etwas sagen, scheute nicht davon zurück, sogar mit gut gesonnenen Kollegen
zu hadern, wenn etwas nicht nach ihren Vorstellungen lief. Ich wusste es aus ihren eigenen
Erzählungen und aus denen anderer Kollegen. Auch unsere Wege gingen irgendeinmal
auseinander. Nachdem sie mir im Sommer 2001 angeboten hatte, einen Kongress des WIP
zum Thema "Human Creativity in the onto-poiesis of Life" zusammen mit dem Institut für
Axiologische Forschungen in Wien zu organisieren und ich schon einiges in die Wege
geleitet hatte, sagte sie die Konferenz unerwartet ab. Der Grund dafür war, dass sie für die
Veranstaltung wesentlich mehr Gelder von österreichischer Seite verlangte als es möglich
war aufzutreiben. Die Zeiten seit 1994, als sie eine Konferenz in Graz veranstaltete, hatten
sich geändert, man sparte an allen Ecken und Enden. Obwohl Kardinal Schönborn, zu dem
ich sie auf eine Audienz begleitete, sehr höflich und zuvorkommend war, schien sie auch
von ihm mehr erwartet zu haben. "Er hat mich nicht zum Essen eingeladen. Der Papst ladet
mich immer zum Essen ein, wenn ich in Rom bin" – sagte sie ein wenig betrübt. "Aber
Ana-Teresa, er hat so viel zu tun, er muss gerade eine Delegation empfangen. Es ist ein
Wunder, dass er sich trotzdem die Zeit genommen hat. Und überhaupt, Wien ist nicht
Rom", erwiderte ich. Und so wählte sie dann Rom, denn in Italien hatte sie wahrlich eine
viel bessere Basis für die Veranstaltung als an der Universität Wien.

Man kann Ana-Teresas Vorgangsweise mögen oder nicht, aber sie war nun einmal
eine Führungspersönlichkeit. Sie wollte von Niemandem abhängen, Niemandem Untertan
sein, und gründete deshalb ihr eigenes Institut. Während viele bemüht waren eine Universi-
tätskarriere zu machen, hatte sie schon von Anfang an verstanden, dass Frauen auch in den

USA viel weniger als Männer verdienen und auch sonst schlechter gestellt sind. Die großen Pläne, die sie schmiedete, hätten niemals realisiert werden können, wenn sie nicht ihre Professorenstelle aufgegeben und sich vollkommen selbstständig gemacht hätte. Manche sehen das als Schwäche an, für mich persönlich zeugt es aber für das was sie in Wirklichkeit war – eine starke Persönlichkeit. Dass sie nicht nur "führen" wollte, sondern auch tatsächlich Führungsqualitäten und einen "praktischen Sinn" besaß, sieht man insbesondere an ihren organisatorischen Tätigkeiten. Sie schaffte es, was andere vor ihr nicht geschafft haben, nämlich der Phänomenologie eine *weltweite Plattform* zu geben. Sie brachte Phänomenologen aus der ganzen Welt zusammen, veranstaltete Diskussionen über neue Zusammenhänge wie "Chinesische Philosophie und Lebensphänomenologie" oder "Islamische Philosophie und Westliche Phänomenologie in Dialog", baute Beziehungen zwischen Philosophen, Künstlern, Wissenschaftlern und Theologen auf und war bemüht die Phänomenologie sowohl in theoretischer Hinsicht, als auch in Form einer Anwendungsmethode in den verschiedensten Gebieten voranzutreiben. Dazu kamen auch ihre hohen wissenschaftlichen Ansprüche. Wenn sie eine Phänomenologie-Konferenz organisierte, dann bestimmte sie nicht nur das Thema, sondern forderte auch, dass man es in einem gewissen Rahmen entwickelte, den sie vorgab. So ist sie auch bei der Übersetzung ins Englische von Karol Wojtyłas *Osoba i Czin* (engl. *The Acting Person,* siehe Wojtyła 1979) vorgegangen als sie sich in seinen Text direkt einmischte. Sie erzählte mir, sie hätte mit ihm einige Zeit, kurz bevor er zum Papst gewählt wurde, in ihrem Haus in Pomfret verbracht und sein Buch "gänzlich überarbeitet", sprich "terminologisch und konzeptuell auf solide philosophisch-phänomenologische Basis gestellt". Sie war sehr stolz darauf und sprach kaum über den Skandal, der nach der Veröffentlichung folgte. Denn dieser Texteingriff führte zu einem langwierigen Rechtsstreit mit dem Vatikan, der eine Kommission mit der Prüfung der Übersetzung beauftragte. Folglich entzog der Vatikan Tymieneckas Institut die Publikationsrechte und veranlasste mit dem Segen des Papstes neue Ausgaben und Übersetzungen. Diese Geschichte hat ihre Freundschaft mit Johannes Paul II wohl ziemlich getrübt, denn sie fühlte sich verraten. Aber 1995, als ich in ihrem Landhaus zu Gast war, hatte sie den Vorfall beinahe vergessen. Sie zeigte mir im Garten das kleine Denkmal, das sie zu Ehren seines Arbeitsbesuches errichtet hatte – ein Granitstein mit der Inschrift "Karol Kardinal Wojtyla, Pope John Paul II, visited Oak Ledge Farm, North Pomfret, Vermont, July 24-26 & August 26-30 1976, as the guest of Ana-Teresa Tymieniecka amd Hendrik Houthakker. Anno Domini 1984". Und sie fügte hinzu: "Er hat hier, unter diesem Pflaumenbaum, eine Messe für uns gehalten. Deshalb wurde das Denkmal an demselben Platz aufgebaut. Es hat eine besondere Bedeutung für uns…" Mit "uns" meinte sie sich selbst und ihren Mann, den Ökonomieprofessor aus Harvard Hendrik Houthakker. Ihm hatte sie übrigens sehr viel zu

verdanken, insbesondere seine langjährige finanzielle Unterstützung des WIP und die lie-
bevolle Art und Weise, mit der er sie und die Familie umsorgte.

2. Logos und Anti-Logos: Das philosophische Werk

Dass sie den Papst verehrte war aus ihrem weichen Tonfall leicht zu entnehmen.
Doch hatte diese persönliche Begegnung auch eine religiöse Bedeutung, bzw. eine Auswir-
kung auf ihre philosophischen Schriften? Schon 1993, auf dem Weltkongress für Philosophie in Moskau, hatte ich sie auf einige Glaubensfragen hin angesprochen. Ich hatte ihr
unter anderem die Frage gestellt, ob die kosmische Vernunft, die sie voraussetzte, eine neue
Art Pantheismus darstelle. Sie wies den Begriff "Pantheismus" vehement zurück und erklärte mir, dass es hier nicht um Gott, sondern um das Leben gehe – das Leben selbst würde
in sich die Vernunft tragen, jedoch nicht als Rationalität oder als Intelligibilität, wie es beim
menschlichen Bewusstsein der Fall sei, sondern als Kreativität nach gewissen Regeln, als
Harmonisierung der vitalen Kräfte. Später sagte ich ihr dann in einem persönlichen Gespräch: "Sie scheinen wohl nicht an Gott zu glauben. Das Leben ist alles und alles ist schon
im Leben, bzw. in der Natur. Das Religiöse ist nur eine Art Anti-Logos, eine menschliche
Erfindung, die aus dem reinen Verlangen nach einer höheren Realität entspringt.[1] Das alles
klingt sehr materialistisch". Diese Bemerkung traf sie wie ein Stich: "Aber nein!" – erwiderte sie. "Ich bin auch gläubig…" Sie dachte ein wenig nach wie sie das nun erklären sollte und fügte hinzu: "Ich glaube schon an eine göttliche Bestimmung. Einmal bei einer Messe hat der Papst sich mir zugewandt und mich sehr seltsam angeschaut. Es war als wollte er
mir sagen, dass ich eine besondere Mission habe".

Ob sie wirklich religiös war, daran zweifle ich auch heute noch. Aber ich bin über-
zeugt, dass sie an ihrer philosophischen Bestimmung, an ihre "Mission", schon seit ihrer
Studienzeit glaubte und, dass nicht einmal der Papst sie von dem eingeschlagenen Weg
hätte abbringen können. Ganz im Gegenteil, so wie sie die Gedanken seines Buches redi-

---

[1] Tymienecka spricht von drei Wege der Selbst-Interpretation-in-der-Existenz: "These are: first, the
"poetic logos," which presides over the creative work of man proper, and through which man estab-
lishes the cornerstones of his human existence; third (the third tableau), in extreme opposition to the
poetic logos, the "spiritual" anti-logos, which, in a swing contrary to man's highest self-creative aspi-
rations, seeks to discover/invent the "ultimate reality" in a process of dissolving the ties projected by
the first; and centrally, the tableau that is in the middle, the second, where the works of the creatively
orchestrated intellect transmute the plurivocal insights, project syncretic unities, and establish the
outlines of its plurirational operational system with a skeleton of structures, regulations, and principles. It is this discursive modality of the intellect's works that allows us to re-construct the mecha-
nisms of man's self-interpretation-in-existence" (Tymieniecka 1988a, p. XXIX).

giert hatte, so interpretierte sie auch Husserl, Conrad-Martius, Ingarden, Merleau-Ponty und andere Phänomenologen, mit dem Ziel, die Phänomenologie auf ihre eigene Art und Weise neu zu begründen. Die Originalität ihres Projekts zeichnet sich unter anderem dadurch aus, dass sie das Leben als eine kreative und rationale Kraft, als eine Art Weltlogos ausgelegt und dadurch eine Variante der Lebensphänomenologie ausgearbeitet hat, die sich wesentlich von dem Lebensverständnis Heideggers und, demzufolge, auch von der *phénoménologie de la vie* eines Michel Henry unterscheidet. An dieser Stelle scheiden sich natürlich die Geister, was allzu verständlich ist in Anbetracht der Entwicklungsgeschichte der phänomenologischen Bewegung, die sich von Anfang an durch den Streit rivalisierenden "Meister" und Schulrichtungen entfaltet hat. Ich selbst habe *Logos and Life* in gewisser Hinsicht kritisch beleuchtet. Zu meiner großen Überraschung hat Tymieniecka diese Kritik respektvoll gewürdigt, indem sie meinen Artikel vom Französischen ins Englische übersetzen und drucken ließ (siehe Raynova/Tymieniecka 1998, 107-116).

In diesem Aufsatz wollte ich, erstens, zeigen, worin sich ihr Projekt von dem von Husserls unterscheidet und, zweitens, dass gerade das Konzept der *Imaginatio Creatrix*, auf welchem sie die Phänomenologie aufbaut, die Ambiguität der Existenz zum Vorschein bringt und somit auch die destruktiven Kräfte der menschlichen Kreativität. Mit anderen Worten, ihre harmonische Sicht der Welt und der Lebenswelt störte mich, ich fand sie übertrieben poetisch und realitätsfern. Zu dem kam, dass ich schon in meinem Buch *Von Husserl zu Ricoeur. Der phänomenologische Zugang zum Menschen* (Raynova 1993), den Logos in einem christologischen Sinn interpretiert hatte, der in die Richtung von Edith Steins *Endliches und ewiges Sein* wies und somit ganz anders war als Tymienieckas Logos-Konzept.

Was Tymienieckas Lebensphänomenologie von der Husserlschen Phänomenologie primär unterscheidet ist, dass sie gerade dort anfängt, wo er einst aufgehört hatte. In seinen Pariser Vorträgen suchte Husserl, wie bekannt, nach einem Archimedischen Punkt, der seiner Philosophie als universelle Wissenschaft zu einer absoluten Begründung verhelfen würde (Husserl 1963, 43). Von der Apodiktizität des Cogito ausgehend, entwickelte er eine transzendentale Theorie der objektiven Welt, die durch die Deskription der universellen Konstitution und der Reduktion zu dem Seinssinn der Welt als ein *Für-jedermann-da* vordringen sollte (ebd., 124). Dieses Projekt wurde jedoch nie zu Ende gebracht, Husserl gab es als "naiv" auf, was später dem Anti-Fundationalismus Tür und Tor öffnete. Tymienieckas Lebensphänomenologie griff hingegen die Idee der Philosophie als *mathesis universalis* erneut auf, schlug aber einen entgegengesetzten Weg ein. Was sie in Frage stellte war nicht Husserls Idee einer absoluten Begründung, sondern seinen philosophischen Ausgangspunkt. Sie erklärt dies zu Beginn von *Logos and Life* folgendermaßen:

> In brief, I propose that the access to the Archimedean point from which, alone, the unity of all the possible perspectives on human experience can be explained, and the key to the Human Condition be obtained, lies in the creative act of the human being which makes him "human" – the creative act of man where the differentiating factors of the macrocosm of life differentiate. (Tymieniecka 1988a, 6)

Indem sie das Cogito durch den kreativen Akt ersetzt, öffnet Tymieniecka das, was sie "die Büchse der Pandora" nennt, nämlich das Reservoir aller Bedeutungen, die der Mensch seiner Umwelt und sich selbst zu geben vermag. Was die Philosophie uns auf diese Weise enthüllt, ist nicht mehr die universelle Struktur der Welt und der Lebenswelt, sondern eine Polyphonie von Lebenswelten, die individuell "orchestriert" werden, je nach der eigenen Entwicklung des Individuums. Von da aus schlägt Tymieniecka eine neue Einteilung der menschlichen Fähigkeiten vor: (a) der poetische Logos, (b) der Intellekt und (c) der spirituelle Anti-Logos, wobei die zentrale Rolle nicht mehr dem Intellekt, sondern der *kreativen Imagination* zukommt (ebd., 11). Diese Einteilung zeigt den Gegensatz zwischen der kreativen Aktivität und der konstitutiven Tätigkeit des Bewusstseins auf und betont die Bewegung vom Allgemeinen zum Partikularen, von der Opazität zur Luzidität, kurz "*from Eros to Logos, whose union presides over the passage from a present life-world to possible worlds*" (ebd., 39). Zugleich erscheint der Mensch in der kreativen Erfahrung als ein Lebewesen unter anderen, was wiederum auf die Einheit-alles-Lebendigen (the unity-of-everything-there-is-alive) hindeutet. Aus dieser Perspektive heraus wird die sonderbare Situation des Menschen als ein Produkt der Evolution der Lebensformen verstanden. Dies eröffnet der Phänomenologie ein viel breiteres Forschungsfeld als die Husserlsche Wesensforschung, nämlich "das Feld des *Bios* und des kosmischen Lebens" (Raynova/Tymieniecka 1995, 87-88).

Es besteht kein Zweifel, dass diese Post-Husserlsche Wende ganz neue Perspektiven ermöglicht. Mit Tymieniecka (und auch mit Marx) kann ich sehr wohl die Idee der kreativen Tätigkeit als "Prototyp des menschlichen Handelns" annehmen. Unsere Wege teilen sich aber bei der Auffassung der Kreativität. Für Tymieniecka stellt der kreative Akt etwas vollkommen Positives dar. Auch wenn sie behauptet, dass die Kreativität durch Konflikte entsteht, so ist sie dennoch die Kraft, welche jede Weiterentwicklung vorantreibt (Tymieniecka 1988a, 56, 70). Dies blendet jedoch die Ambiguität der menschlichen Existenz (im Sartreschen und im Beauvoirschen Sinne) und die dunklen Seiten des Handelns (das Böse nach Ricœur) komplett aus. Die Kreativität mag innovativ sein, wie Tymieniecka an diversen Stellen behauptet (ebd., 73ff), doch dies bedeutet nicht, dass jede Erfindung zum Guten beiträgt. Menschen können sehr kreativ sein beim Denunzieren, Foltern, Verunstalten oder Töten. Sind tödliche Medikamente, Waffen, Foltermethoden usw. nicht auch Produkte derselben *imaginatio creatrix*, die sie als die erhabenste Fähigkeit des Menschen preist? Gerade die menschliche Kreativität weist auf unsere Ambiguität hin und zeugt von der Notwendigkeit das Humane vom Inhumanen zu unterscheiden. Anders gesagt – und das ist, was ich Tymieniecka damals vorgeschlagen habe –, es wäre vonnöten ein anderes Konzept des Anti-Logos einzuführen; eines, das den Anti-Logos nicht als Spiritualität, sondern als Monstrosität thematisiert, als bewusste Verletzung sozialer Regeln oder "kosmischer Gesetze", als gewollten Missbrauch oder Vernichtung des Anderen. Die Heilige Schrift spricht diese Phänomene mehrfach an, sie zeigt, dass der Logos und der Anti-Logos zwei entgegengesetzte Kräfte in uns und außerhalb von uns sind, deren Kampf die ganze menschliche Geschichte durchzieht.

Ich habe mit Tymieniecka über dieses Thema schon im ersten Interview lange debattiert. Sie war nicht jemand der leicht nachgab. Und aus der Position heraus, die sie schon entwickelt hatte und an der sie fest hielt, konnte sie auch nicht anders. In dem engen Bezug zwischen Logos und *Imaginatio Creatrix*, den sie hergestellt hatte, war kein Platz für das Böse und das Hässliche, sondern nur für das Gute und das Erhabene:

> Wenn ich eine so große Bedeutung den Leidenschaften beimesse, so ist es, weil ich die Aktivität des Logos aufzeigen möchte, der sie mit Hilfe der Kreativität transformiert. Gerade der Logos gibt den Emotionen Bedeutung und Sinn, er verwandelt sie in einen erhabenen Sinn. Somit kommt der Logos zum Vorschein und nicht die Kreativität. Die Kreativität kooperiert mit dem Logos auf mehrere Weisen. Erstens, sie wirkt als Inspiration. Zweitens, sie wirkt, indem sie ein Netz von unendlichen Möglichkeiten zur Verfügung stellt. Und, drittens, sie stellt die Bezüge zwischen den verschiedenen Elementen des Logos her, die sonst niemals in eine Einheit und Harmonie verbunden werden könnten (Raynova/Tymieniecka 1995, 98).

3. Ein würdiges Vermächtnis

Unabhängig davon, wie man die Person und auch das philosophische Werk von Ana-Teresa Tymieniecka bewerten mag, es steht für mich außer Zweifel, dass mit ihr die phänomenologische Bewegung eine wichtige Figur und ein Stück lebendiger Phänomenologie-Geschichte verloren hat. Mit ihrer gigantischen Tätigkeit als Herausgeberin hat sie, einerseits, die Vielfalt der Bereiche und der methodologischen Anwendungsmöglichkeiten der Phänomenologie aufgezeigt und sichtbar gemacht und, andererseits, den Versuch unternommen, die phänomenologischen Forschungen möglichst breit, ja weltweit zu erfassen. Einen wichtigen Beitrag in dieser Hinsicht stellt die Veröffentlichung von Enzyklopädien und Nachschlagewerken bei Springer dar. Auch ihre philosophischen Schriften verdienen einen speziellen Platz im Rahmen der post-husserlschen Weiterentwicklung der Phänomenologie. Sie hätten sicherlich mehr Beachtung gefunden, wenn sie von einem Mann geschrieben worden wären, der an einem Lehrstuhl in Harvard oder in Cambridge unterrichtet hätte. Dennoch, ihr "praktischer Sinn" hat ihr dazu verholfen, das Problem mit der Weiterführung des World Phenomenology Institute auf eine wunderbare Art zu lösen. Im Jahr 2008 konnte sie ihren Briefwechsel mit Karol Wojtyła/Johannes Paul II, der Hunderte von Briefen enthält, an die Polnische Nationalbibliothek für eine beachtliche Summe verkaufen. Damit wurde das WIP materiell abgesichert. Ob der Nachlass ihrer Briefe genauso wichtig ist, wie ihre philosophischen Werke, darüber wird die Zukunft entscheiden. Hoffen wir, dass die erwartete Veröffentlichung genug Aufsehen erregen wird, um auch ihren philosophischen Beitrag in Erinnerung zu rufen.

Prof. Dr. Yvanka B. Raynova, Institute for the Study of Societies and Knowledge –
Bulgarian Academy of Sciences, Sofia / Institut für Axiologische Forschungen, Wien,
raynova[at]iaf.ac.at

Literaturangaben

Husserl, Edmund. *Cartesianische Meditationen*, in *Husserliana*, Bd. 1, The Hague: Martinus Nijhoff, 1963.

Raynova, Yvanka B. *Ot Huserl do Rikjor. Fenomenologicheskiiat podhod kym choveka* (*Von Husserl bis Ricoeur: Der phänomenologische Zugang zum Menschen*), Sofia: University Publishing House "St. Kl. Okhridski", 1993.

Raynova, Yvanka B./Tymieniecka, Ana-Teresa. "Ana-Teresa Tymieniecka: Kreativnijat opit v svetlinata na fenomenologijata na jivota" ("Ana-Teresa Tymieniecka: Die kreative Erfahrung aus der Sicht der Phänomenologie des Lebens"), in Raynova, Yvanka B. *Filosofiajta v kraja na XX vek* (*Philosophy at the End of the XX Century*), Pleven: EA, 1995, 83-103.

Raynova, Yvanka B. "'The Human "Animal': Prolegomenon to a Phenomenology of Monstrousness."- In: Ana-Teresa Tymienecka (ed.). *The Human "Animal"* (*Analecta Husserliana*, Vol. LVII), Dordrecht / Boston / London / Tokyo: Kluwer Academic Publishers, 1998, 107-116.

Raynova, Yvanka B. "Jean-Paul Sartre: A profound Revision of Husserlian Phenomenology," in A.-T. Tymieniecka (ed.), *Phenomenology World Wide. Foundations - Expanding Dynamics - Life-Engagements*, Dordrecht/Boston /London/Tokyo: Kluwer Academic Publishers, 2002, 323-335.

Tymieniecka, Anna-Teresa. *Logos and Life: Creative Experience and the Critique of Reason*, Book 1, Dordrecht/Boston/London/Tokyo: Kluwer Academic Publishers, 1988a.

Tymieniecka, Anna-Teresa. *Logos and Life: Creative Experience and the Critique of Reason*, Book 2, Dordrecht/Boston/London/Tokyo: Kluwer Academic Publishers, 1988b.

Wojtyła, Karol. *The Acting Person* (*Analecta Husserliana*, Vol. X), Dordrecht / Boston / London / Tokyo: Kluwer Academic Publishers, 1979.

INTERVIEW

At the Sources of the Phenomenology of Life*
An Interview with Ana-Teresa Tymieniecka (Hanover, NH)
by Yvanka B. Raynova (Sofia/Vienna)

Raynova: *Professor Tymieniecka, you had an impressive formation, having such eminent teachers as Roman Ingarden and Józef Bocheński. How much of that formation influenced your own philosophy, or how much do you owe to your masters?*

Tymieniecka: This is a terribly complex question. My interest in philosophy was awakened when I was very young, before even knew the meaning of the word "philosophy." It came out in high school during the class in Latin literature, when our teacher asked for a volunteer to prepare a paper on Horace, more specifically on his "philosophy." I was about fourteen then and did not know the meaning of the word, but fascinated, I volunteered. And as I pondered the verses of Horace and wondered what philosophy might be in them, I sought the help of a remarkable man there in our small town in Poland. This older gentleman walked about dressed in the same clothing summer and winter, never changing its thickness in the cold. He had a long beard and enormous blue eyes. And he walked in a meditative way. He was a private tutor and was considered a "philosopher." Perhaps that was, because of his look. He was for many like Socrates himself. And so I asked a classmate, who took tutoring in German from him, whether he would consent to talk with me so that I could learn from him whether what I thought to be philosophy was philosophy or not. She asked him and he consented. I went to him half trembling. After a good session, he said to me: "Well, that is it exactly; you have already in mind the propaedeutics of philosophy." He then invited me to chat about philosophy. On my next visit he gave me Twardowski's book *Der Gegenstand der Vorstellung*. I found it very difficult to understand. First of all my German was not yet good enough, and then it was a very technical work. But I did not give up, and he gave me other works. He gave me *The Republic* of Plato and portions of the Dialogues. If I expand on this, it

---

* Interviewer's Note: This is my second Interview with Ana-Teresa Tymieniecka, the first one was realized in 1993 at the World Congress of Philosophy in Moscow. This one was recorded one year later, in December 1994, at the World Phenomenology Institute. It was published firstly in Bulgarian, and thereafter in English, on the homepage of the World Phenomenology Institute.

is for two reasons. Twenty-five years later, when I was studying in Switzerland, I discovered that my tutor had been a fellow student of Ingarden in Lvov under Kazimiercz Twardowski. Now, Twardowski himself was a student of Brentano. So when after the war I passed the university entrance examinations and went to study in Kraków and landed in Roman Ingarden's class, there was nothing astonishing in the philosophy he imparted; I was familiar to all. I came to Ingarden and said that all this makes me tremble with excitement, because I had already read and thought about it. But I asked him why he did not speak anymore about ontology. He replied that if he were to talk more about the modes of being, as I wished, the class would be empty. There were 300 in it otherwise! And so, you see, my biding interest from childhood for philosophy, without my knowing exactly what it was, led me to Ingarden and then straight to phenomenology.

Through Twardowski I got from Brentano the basic notions underlying phenomenology. That was the very beginning. I studied under Ingarden for two years, during which I completed the four year philosophy program, something that was made possible immediately in the postwar years. This was done to compensate for the time in which the Germans had closed the universities. From Kraków I went to Switzerland. My father had died when I was nine, and my brother being twenty years older than me was like a father to me. My brother was a hero of the battle for Monte Cassino (the tank unit he led opened the way to Piedimonte). As with the rest of General Anders' army, he could not return to Communist Poland. So he settled in England. He wanted absolutely that I come there. Since our family had established ties in Switzerland, the University of Fribourg being our chosen seat of studies, I landed there. An uncle had been professor and dean there. He had just died, leaving a small inheritance. I went to collect the inheritance, and my brother joined me there. He introduced me to Father Bocheński, who had been his army chaplain. And so it transpired that I remained at Fribourg to study. Thus, a coincidence played a strong role in my career.

Now, I spontaneously gave myself the mission of spreading in the West the knowledge of the work of Ingarden, who was completely unknown abroad. A few scholars such as Jean Wahl did remember meeting him, but they really did not know much about him. Landgrebe and Spiegelberg remembered *Das literarische Kunstwerk*, but that was it. Since I had developed a great affection for my master, I spent ten years making him known. But by the end of that effort I was no longer an Ingardenian. At the beginning, I swore by him, and whenever I befriended a philosopher, I would give him a full-fledged lecture on what Ingarden proposed, on what problems he resolved. I recall particularly such a session with Jean Wahl at a cafe in Paris. But I did not believe anymore in his philosophy. I still thought that he should be better known, but I developed some doubts. Those began actually when I was still in Kraków. I also undertook studies at the Academy of Fine Arts there. I was painting in the morning and going to courses at the university in the afternoon. Ingarden's main course was in aesthetics, a course I took for those two years. His ontology of aesthetics was really the basis for a great deal of his philosophy. I was struck by the discrepancy between the way a philosopher considered a work of art as an observer and the way in which a painter sees it. There was such a radical discrepancy. I started to wonder about the role of creative experience in making a work of art, and so I began to study not only its ideal structure, but also the observer's recovery of that structure. Now, in Switzerland, I was obtaining a double degree in philosophy and French literature. As the subject for my dissertation in French literature I choose the debate on pure poetry between Bremond and Valéry. Now, pure poetry was exactly the gist of creative accomplishment. Thus, I was already undermining in my mind the rigid ontological structure of Ingarden's theory of aesthetics. Later, in Fribourg, I became very skeptical about another point of Ingardenian ontology, which I want to remind here, because that point was also a classic foundation of Husserl's thought in his Göttingen years. Ingarden was Husserl's student and a member of the Göttingen School of phenomenology. He took from Husserl the fundamental intuitions and the eidetic method. And, like some other members of the Göttingen School (such as Reinach, Conrad-Martius, Edith Stein, etc.), he broke with Husserl when the master's focus turned to transcendental consciousness. The rigid phenomenological methodology and the whole framework inherited from Husserl by Ingarden awakened in me serious doubts concerning existence. The Göttingen School suspended existence and also the question of whether an object exists. That was one of the first steps of the phenomenological *epoché*, which was then really taken seriously, the so-called phenomenological reduction. That was the instrument of philosophical work for phenomenology, of phenomenological description. Well, the suspension of existence put me in great doubt, and I wrote a small article, which is somewhat obscure for me now. It was titled "Twenty Real Dollars." This was my first American foray in print. It appeared in *The Monist*. There I voiced radically a call for the recovery of existence against this complete suspension. Now, to tell the truth, at that time this was unheard of in phenomenology. Phenomenology after the Second World War was completely dedicated to the thought of the period of Husserl's *Ideas I*. That was the main work discussed at this time, and then slowly others of Husserl's works, right through his posthumous works, began to be discussed. In *Ideas I* Husserl was still maintaining the strict eidetic suspension of existence. Now, these two points, the need to philosophically appreciate creative experience, on the one hand, and the need to revamp phenomenological formulations to vindicate real existence, on the other, underlay the greening of my own philosophical thought, even before the writing of my doctoral dissertation. It was about the foundations of phenomenology in Ingarden and Hartmann, and I published it as *Essence and Existence* with Aubier. This work already showed that I was directing my thought on essence, or the a priori ideal thing, elsewhere, that I found that the eidetic approach does not suffice. I found that essences cannot be sclerosed, that they are not unchangeable things. From there on I was really going my own way, without knowing that fully yet. My first original published paper – I had previously had articles on Ingarden, on his metaphysics and ethics – was "Eidos, Idea, and Participation," which appeared in *Kantstudien*. When I wrote it I thought that I was exfoliating Ingarden's theory of essence, i.e. his ontology. It was a very tough paper. Ingarden, like Husserl, never spoke on *methexis*, i.e. on how these ideal essences participates in concrete things. This is the great Platonic issue, of course. They had separated real existence from essences, but they could not deny that reality exists. Reality was always there, and from it they were deriving essences. But they never treated the question of the relationship between real existence and essences. So I attacked this question, and I thought that I did so in an Ingardenian way. I then sent Ingarden the manuscript, as we were at that time in intense communication, intensive as much as the handling of the mail between the West and Communist Poland allowed. I received a letter back saying that the thought developed in this paper was my own theory, and that he had never thought in such a way. Well, that was a terrible shock for me –it meant that I was now on my own, by myself, alone. It is so terribly easy to follow in the footsteps of a master, to just exfoliate his thought. But it is totally different to have to think *ab initio*. So I found myself thrown into the air. It was a terrible existential experience. I had to take about thirty footnotes that referred to Ingarden's works out of the paper. I published it without them. From there on I was thinking on my own. The next paper which I published in *Kantstudien* continued this one on the constitutive a priori. Now, Ingarden promised that he would write an answer to the first paper. But he did not. Instead he wrote a special treatise on essences, one which I did not read very carefully, I must say. From there on I was moving towards the vindication of real existence, but vindicating it via the relationship between creativity and the whole creative context. My next publication went far beyond the limits of phenomenology. That was "Prolegomena to the Phenomenology of Cosmic Creation." This was a daring thing, because before, in phenomenology, only Max Scheler delved into cosmic issues, but not into cosmic creation. This piece was well received among experts. Ingarden himself said that it was a very mature work. But he was very angry! He wrote me a letter in which he said that he is annoyed, because I, his student, was now talking about real individuals in philosophy. How, he asked, could I as his student do that? I answered him that in my own thought I actually did not owe that much to his thought. I said that I owed much less him than he owed to Husserl. That exchange was of some importance. Ingarden had visited us before in California and I read then the manuscript of the third volume of his Controversy over the Existence of the World, a volume dealing with the principle of causality, "das Kausalproblem." Later, I heard to my amazement that he was rewriting it. When it appeared three or four years later, and I looked at it, I found that the main focus of the book was the real individual! He introduced this as the heart of his theory, and even italicized the words "real individual" throughout for emphasis. I have never mentioned this – saying it here for the first time to you – but the coincidence can be checked. So, I was entirely on my own then, navigating in the sphere of creative experience. I published *Eros and Logos: Introduction to the creative experience*. There was an opening to cosmology, an opening to reality in the first place, because essences, as I presented them, were creative principles and not eternal and unchangeable models, somehow incarnated in things. Essences, as I saw them, are regulative principles and points of reference, they are not fixed, hardened realities. That was the development of my thinking. We can say that between my childhood and my mature work I went through three phases, at least.

Raynova: *I know that you spend also some years in Paris. What influences could be found in your philosophical work from the time of your studies in France?*

Tymieniecka: Well, first, there was the contrast with Fribourg. Fribourg was a university where a militantly rationalist approach was taken to philosophy. It was a pure Aristotelianism, very rigid, that was taught. But I had there a pied-à-terre in contemporary philosophy. Father Bocheński, a logician, was giving a fascinating series of courses on the history of contemporary philosophy, a particular passion of his. Being a very honest scholar he believed that a historian has to put aside his own thinking and enter into the mind of the philosopher he presents and make the best of it. So there I learned all about the Göttingen School, the Freiburg School, all about Husserl's development, about all sorts of things that I never heard from Ingarden, who presented only his own phenomenology. It was Bocheński, who taught me about the course of Husserl's thought and the thinking of his students, Scheler, etc. Bocheński was really a marvelous man for me, for he was taking me to philosophical meetings. As a driver, he appreciated very much having a map reader along. So he took me to the World Congress at Amsterdam, even I was only a student. There, he introduced me to Bertrand Russell and other prominent figures. He invited also philosophers like Gabriel Marcel to present lectures at Fribourg and then he introduced me to them. He always introduced me as a philosopher. And so at a young age I was already going to Paris two or three times a year to talk with Louis Lavelle and Jean Wahl. Consequently the radical rationalism of Fribourg was challenged by the intense existential thought prevailing in Paris. This contrast and challenge was very important for my development. I mentioned Lavelle. He was not an existentialist at all but a pure metaphysician, a spiritualist. And so I was pulled in various directions which made me more and more delineate and clarify my own thinking.

Raynova: *In sum, was it Ingarden's and Husserl's suspension of the problem of existence through the method of reduction that led you to the Phenomenology of Life?*

Tymieniecka: I mentioned my orientation toward creativity, the expansion of phenomenology to reality and to the cosmos. These were my points of reference. These were the points from which my framework was elaborated. You are asking me about Husserl and Ingarden, but it was not simply these authors that I read. I was reading practically all of the phenomenologists of the Göttingen School. And then, when Heidegger's works began to be more disputed after the war, I read all his works, everything that he published. And, as I said, I was involved in discussions with existential thinkers. Of course, I read also everything of Sartre, and of Merleau-Ponty. So I was developing philosophically in a rather large orbit, and was not just continuing Ingarden or Husserl. There is also another perspective in which my readings were important for the development of my thought. I was dealing also with literature. I received a second doctorate in French literature. And in Fribourg I also studied with some intensity Slavic literature, and continued to be interested in the plastic arts and music. I no longer painted or played, because the lack of time. At the same time I developed a fascination with another line of phenomenological inquiry, a quite natural extension of phenomenology, namely psychology. From Piaget's psychological study of the development of the child you can move to Husserl's picture of the genesis of consciousness. Binswanger moved phenomenology in the direction of psychiatry. I developed a great interest in the human sciences, too. My thought was not shaped only by the digestion of philosophy, but became a wider basis encompassing the fine arts, literature, the human sciences, etc. Now, if you would ask me how I understand phenomenology and philosophy, I would give as an example an intermediary work that I published; it was my first work in English language, which shows how my thought has unfolded from thereon. That was *Phenomenology and Science in Contemporary European Thought*, published in 1960 by Farrar, Straus and Giroux in New York. It came out in hardback and paperback and was an instant success. It was used as an introductory text in phenomenology at colleges, even at a seminar in psychology at Harvard, and so the first printing of 10,000 sold out in a year. It was translated into Japanese right away, and a new edition came out there a few years ago. I have been asked many times to revise it for translation. It was a novelty then to write on the influence of phenomenology in the sciences. There was an influence from the very beginning of phenomenology, but it had not been much written about it. After my book appeared there was a stream of articles, essays, and books on the subject. So, if it were to come out in new translations, I would have to revise it to take into consideration all that has been said since. But for that I've never had time. In this little book of about 220 pages, I analyze the influence of phenomenology precisely in the human sciences and aesthetics, which covers a large ground of human investigation, and that is how I understand phenomenology. Let us remember, that Husserl's first intent was to establish phenomenology as a *mathesis universalis,* just like Leibniz's universal science, i.e. as a fundamental groundwork from which all human knowledge can be explicated, and in which all human knowledge can find its roots. Well, this little book of mine shows the steps of my thinking in that direction. However, in order to frame a *mathesis universalis* Husserl had first to abandon the regional ontologies he had undertaken by applying his *epoché*. He concluded that the *epoché* did not take him to the ultimate foundation. As we know, he then entered into the realms of consciousness as the ultimate foundation and from there he moved on to the *Lebenswelt* as the last foundation. But the *Lebenswelt*, if you analyze it clearly, cannot be the last foundation either. To make phenomenology a universal science one has to go much deeper than Husserl did, and one cannot stop at any phase of his proposal. He himself was changing his proposal as he went along, and at no stage did it prove to be satisfactory. Thus, I had to develop. Well, I naturally was digging, and finally I struck at the real stream of all rationality, because that is what was really in question. As you remember, Leibniz took the universal characteristic to be the rational axiom for all foundations. In radical contrast to Leibniz, I found the foundation for all rationality in the development of life. Here we are. I have since developed a phenomenology of life which is meant to be a *mathesis universalis* for all natural sciences, for all the human sciences, and also for all human knowledge.

> **Raynova:** *I see, but how do you understand Life?*

> **Tymieniecka:** This is an impossible question. We say "as large as life." With life comes everything. But the point at which I struck the key to the Pandora's box of life was the point at which I realized that there is no life without self-individualization. The dynamic process of life is not topsy-turvy. The elements of life do not coalesce and inter-generate at random, whimsically, as Bergson would have it. It does not unfold without any direction or constraint or element of proportion. To the contrary, here is a self-individualizing process in which life forms itself in accordance with an entelechial code.

> **Raynova:** *You are about to finish a paper, which is the final part of the forth volume of* Logos and Life. *Could you outline the most important points of this final work?*

> **Tymieniecka:** To be exact, I have now finished four different papers, not just one on this subject. Together they will go into the fourth volume of my book *Logos and Life*; they mark my progress, my advance. Now, to answer your question in a way that would relate to what I have said by now, in the three volumes of *Logos and Life* already published, I have laid down the foundation for a phenomenological investigation of life, which means the uncovering of a completely new field of research. It is not that a field on which life could be investigated had already been prepared by philosophy or by phenomenology in particular. Precisely not. Maybe Husserl had advanced the furthest by talking of the *Lebenswelt*, in which the world and life somewhat interact, but that is not far enough. The question still remains, namely which are the reasons for the particular forms of the world that we can find only in the

principles of life per se. So, you see, these principles, which Leibniz – in another context and while having another end in view – called using an excellent term "the inner workings of nature," have to be uncovered. When we manage to engineer an entrance into the inner workings of nature and then slowly realize the main bearings for such an inquiry, then we can truly pursue it. This inquiry is not like the phenomenal world around us that we investigate at first hand, it is not like the mathematical world in which we start with a first theorem and then unroll everything else. It is something that had not been done in philosophy and which needs a complete beginning, an uncovering. The phenomenal world, the world of the manifestation of life, I likened to clothing on a body. From those clothes, magnificent as they may be, we do not see what the body is like and how it functions. In the first volume of *Logos and Life*, which is the most substantial, I uncovered these inner workings of nature, entering into them through an examination of the creative experience. In the creative experience of man, it is precisely the way in which we can enter the inner workings of life. In the second volume, I showed that life in its marvelous self-individualizing development culminates in the inventive, creative unfolding of life with the human being. But then there comes the point where the human being asks about the ultimate unfolding of life, or the ultimate sense of it. All goes along the line of the formation of sense. And then, in the pursuit of this ultimate question, there is an undoing of this marvelous creative work that has been established as that pursuit spins something which I call the transnatural destiny of the soul, until it spins away from the logos of life altogether. In the third book, I showed how self-individualization unfolds in a specifically human way, that is, in culture. Now, what I have done in these four new papers is this: in two of them I have gone through the analyses of Husserl and Merleau-Ponty to show that these analyses indicate that there is precisely a level of the inner workings of life without which their analyses would hang in the air. They themselves do not reach the point of entering into the inner workings of life, but without going that further step we cannot understand the meaning of terms like "the flesh of the world" in Merleau-Ponty, or see how the genealogy of logic of Husserl is really rooted in experience. In the third paper, I have entered on something quite particular. We are now dealing with issues in our society that only philosophy can deal with. As Bertrand Russell said, philosophy always develops in relation to the actual problems of the world. Philosophy does not develop just in the discussions of scholars. It always reflects the consciousness of a culture. Now, one of the great problems that pervades all human civilization today is that of ethics. There are ecoethics, bioethics, social ethics. We read about them in the newspapers all the time, but they are completely without any direction. All of these ethics just "beat around the bush," as Americans say, they don't touch the real point. So, in a paper that I read at the *Entretien* of the International Institute of Kyoto in September, I proposed that the crucial thing for civilization is to find the measure of things. In ethics you cannot talk about principles and norms of behavior unless you find a measure by means of which these principles and rules should be distributed. Whether it is justice, honesty, sincerity, or whatever, there will be always the need to measure its degree. The great question is the question of measure. This is what we have completely lost amidst our marvelous technological progress. That progress has somewhat caught human beings unprepared, and we have such a difficulty adjusting our conception of life, personal life and social life, to these changes. We have no orientation. We don't know what to expect, or what we should expect and strive for. So for all this it is an absolute necessity that we grasp the measure in things. And so I have proposed in a deep swing into my philosophy that the principles of measure can be found in life itself through self-individualization in existence. The model of self-individualization fits every field, whether it be the study of the inorganic, the organic, bios or zoe, gregarious life, social and cultural life, at each step of the unfolding a measure is intrinsic. So we do have an enormously diversified and yet coherent ladder of measurement precisely in the model of self-individualization in existence. And so I have proposed this for the physical sciences, as well as for the human sciences. The biological sciences are in enormous need of an axis about which to organize their research. It is being done in a fragmentary way. Nothing is known in any of the biological sciences about the inner workings of the whole. There is no orientation. The principle of self-individualization, which I have developed at length in my explorations, is the key to finding measure amid our present disarray. The fourth paper, which I will be presenting at the upcoming American Philosophical Association, Eastern Division Meeting will address the origins of rationality. Measure can be found at all levels of life, since each level presents a certain type or modality of rationality. So the whole investigation of life is the investigation of the genesis of rational articulations. I am going to present in the line of the genealogy of logic the relationship between experience, especially sensory experience, and the function of logical judgment. Husserl assumed – it was one of his revolutionary thoughts – that there is continuity between experience and judgment, and that, as Kant said, there cannot be experience without judgment and judgment without experience. Husserl actually went much further than Kant, due to the fact that he demonstrated the truth of this in detail. But I consider Husserl's investigation insufficient, because when he introduces transcendental consciousness as the factor of judgment, he does not know in function of what transcendental consciousness is capable of taking further steps than empirical life and its experience. So I am proposing a new idea of how it is possible that with judgment we enter into the specifically human creative realm.

  Raynova: *You say that there is a need of orientation in the biological sciences, and, if I understand you rightly, it is philosophy, in particular the Phenomenlogy of Life, which could give them the key. But actually, with the boom of scientific rationality, with the pronounced*

"death" of the Subject, the "end" of the grand narratives, or even with the "end" of History,
many people (scholars, intellectuals, politicians) don't see any necessity of philosophy as
academic discipline. In that context, what is (for you) philosophy, and why still we need it?

Tymieniecka: In our days, the practice of philosophy is in great decadence, because
the majority of the present-day philosophers, who occupy the attention of the world, are rela-
tivists. They relativize philosophy to just a special activity of the mind and give up philosophy's principle vocation. The vocation of philosophy in the West from the time of the ancient
Greeks has been that of answering the questions that no other branch of knowledge can answer. Scientific inquiry, the fine arts, letters have proved incapable of answering some questions. Each branch of knowledge is always striving toward some most general principles and
toward understanding reality in terms of these principles. But philosophy today is giving up
this quest. Its purview is divided into small fields such as analysis of language, and hermeneutic procedures. It is just a dialectical occupation. I am audacious enough in this "dürftige
Zeit", as Heidegger put it, to maintain the real vocation of philosophy. I ask: Why are things
as they are? Why is life as it is? Why do human beings strive in such a way and not another?
Answering these questions is the vocation of philosophy. Doing it means to go to the roots of
human thinking and acting. Now, if you ask me how the phenomenology of life can fulfill this
vocation, well, as I have already indicated to you, it descends to the inner workings of nature
through the creative act of the human being and not trough the cognitive act that philosophy
has focused on for centuries. In the creative act, man is the doer and he is dealing with the
inner workings of nature as they related to him and to all other human and living beings. This
is what I call the unity-of-everything-that- is-alive. It is through the creative act one can de-
scend to this deepest plane on which everything is being played. However, how can we do
justice to all of the regions of knowledge in this field? Unfortunately, philosophy is sifting
through everything by applying the *epoché* or by using some other method converting philosophy in a distilled agglomerate of our knowledge. This has been the bias of the majority of
philosophers in the West. If this reduction was not achieved through the transcendental reduction, it has been done by reducing everything to the level of empirical sensuous knowledge.
Or, it was a purely mathematical approach that was taken, or a completely spiritualistic one.
In the West, the proposal of each philosopher has involved some major bias, a limited "cor-
rect" perspective within which all life and all human acts, attitudes, and comprehension are to
be viewed. I totally disclaim any bias of this sort, because in the creative act we necessarily
confront all of the perspectives/modalities of living beings in the unity-of-everything-that- is-
alive. How, though, when I have said that our approach is an interdisciplinary *mathesis*
universalis, can we deal with the givenness of sociological life, the givenness of the artistic
life, or the givenness of the life of empirical research in a way that puts all together? Here I

return to Husserl's great "principle of all principles," as he called it. He did not follow this principle in a thorough-going way, for in one life one cannot do it. The "principle of all principles" says that every type of experience whether it is sensory, whether it is imaginative, whether it is remembrance, or a projection of hopes, whether it is a mathematical intuition, it is equally worthy of philosophical treatment, provided that each of these types is treated in its proper way. That is, mathematical experience has to be approached in a way proper to mathematics, psychological life in a way proper to psychology, etc. The nub here is that each type of experience has to be apprehended, to be "heard", and registered in its own language. As the Germans say: "Hier liegt der Hund begraben." We cannot in the same language treat experiences that have little in common; a strictly rational reflection, for example, cannot be treated in the same way as aesthetic sensitivity and sublimation. So each type of experience necessitates its own approach, or "ear", and cannot be reduced to some other as has been done throughout the whole history of philosophy. We have made these reductions in quest of a unified field. This was the task of the philosophers of the past. It is just the opposite that I am doing; I am giving a specific "hearing" to each type of experience and inventing for each a special language. My phenomenology of life uses five languages. First, I use a strictly scholarly matter-of-fact language for reflection, for reasoning. Then I use an aesthetic, literary, poetic language for the things of the fine arts, of poetry, and aesthetics. I have a common sense language for treating sensuous experience. In addition, I have an extremely refined conjectural language, which I use when I make a strict description and when I move from it to conclusions at a higher level. My cosmological work has been done on the basis of conjectural inference. Basing myself on the phenomenological essential analysis of reality, I have been seeking the points where this reality points to explanation. And so, by conjectural inference, I have postulated from these indications at a higher level an explanation of the reality. Finally, I have a special language for the phenomenology of the sacred. No matter what convictions we may have, no matter what our attitudes are in this respect, even if we be deaf to religious experiences and the spiritual life, just as some are deaf to music, or insensitive to aesthetic experience, we cannot dismiss spiritual experiences. This type of experience is universal. Everyone can potentially have one. We cannot speak directly of spiritual experiences, though, of the spiritual genesis of the human being that all are capable of, and the greatest majority develops in some way. Yet another, most complex language is needed to do justice to these experiences. The second volume of my *Logos and Life – The Three Movements of the Soul –* is devoted to this.

Raynova: *Let us focus on the relation between the Phenomenology of Life and the Sacred. You say that we need a "more complex language" in order to apprehend and to* *explain religious experience, i.e. the phenomena of religious life. Would this imply the elaboration of a new religious philosophy using the phenomenological approach to life?*

Tymieniecka: Well, I have to say categorically no, because the way in which I understand philosophy tells me that philosophy has to know its own limits. Philosophy, as we know, especially with Husserl, has to be self-legitimizing, that is, its procedure has to be legitimized by the standards of thought itself. Religion, religious life, religious experience, religious phenomenon do not belong to the same rational framework to which philosophy belongs. Philosophy can legitimize itself only within a certain rational framework, which is the rational framework of life. Actually, the phenomenology of life that I have developed is at the same time a critique of reason, a critique of reason in the sense that I am radically counteracting the idea that there is one reason, the reason of the human mind, which is held up as the measure of whatever happens in nature. I say to the contrary that the human mind is only one among an infinite number of rationalities. The whole realm of life through its different phases, beginning with pre-life, then passing to organic life, then to the zooidal realm, advances through rational articulations that belong to the nature of life itself. Life is projecting an enormous network of rational articulations, some limited to events, or to functions, others being processes. These projected rationalities could be compared to the thread spun by a spider, along which the spider can then walk. Just so, these rationalities carry life. All of these rationalities of life together with the rationalities fulgurating out of the human mind, which also proceed from life, form a rational field. But the whole point of a religious creed is that it transcends this framework. The question of the divine transgresses the limits of life, it launches beyond, to the radically Other, the radically different. Consequently, if phenomenology, as I envision it, is supposed to encompass the whole field of rationalities relative to life, then religion is beyond it, and it could not be grasped by philosophy in a way proper to philosophy. However, as I pointed out, philosophy cannot ignore religious experience, just as it cannot ignore any other experience. It is capable to articulate religion's development and to illuminate its significance, up to a certain point. Beyond that point, where it is a question of transcendence, there is a limit.

Raynova: *One last question. What motivated you to leave the University career and to found the World Phenomenology Institute?*

Tymieniecka: This final question might have been more properly asked in the middle of this interview. For when I founded the World Phenomenology Institute, it was out of a profound need to be able, in conversation with a community of scholars, to develop my initial intuitions and ideas, which I could not do at a university. I had taught for twenty years at seven American universities and one in Canada, teaching mostly graduate students preparing their doctoral dissertations. This should mean that one can engage in regular philosophical conversation. Well, this is not the case. I never could have advanced my thought in that setting, for a serious teacher is concerned to impart the very basics for the students' own sake. A teacher owes first allegiance to his or her students. So I decided after those twenty years to form a true community of scholars. And we can say that from 1968 on, my thought has developed together with the Institute since the themes discussed proceed from my own questions, the development of which is advanced by the work and the discussions of the scholars, out of which new interests are generated. While through our seminars, symposia, and conferences there runs a strong leitmotif, each scholar does what he or she wants, and so the Institute advances philosophically. It is a reciprocal work. My thought would not have advanced as well as it has, had it not been for this interaction within the community of the Institute. The Institute affords scholars the opportunity to focus on their principal interests and, especially, on what they may not be able to discuss with their colleagues at their institutions, given some political concerns. Here they can speak their soul out and be listened to with respect and attention. It is precisely this core idea that our aim is the progress of philosophy which attracts scholars from around the world. It has now attracted scholars from fifty-eight countries. And there is always a new generation coming. We are now working with a third generation of Japanese phenomenologists as well as with a third generation of Chinese scholars, who have come very quickly to phenomenology, practically in no time, just in twenty years. I am not even mentioning the French, where you can see that we are attracting already the fourth generation. They stream to us, because they see that here is a forum where they can grow expansively in their thinking, and to be truly appreciated and respected. In brief, it is the very personal interest in the problems of philosophy that can flourish here, and that is the main point of our Institute.